I0605772

UNITED STATES

BY MARIE JASKULKA

Essential Library
An Imprint of Abdo Publishing
abdobooks.com

ABDOBOOKS.COM
Published by Abdo Publishing, a division of ABDO, PO Box 398166, Minneapolis, Minnesota 55439.

Printed in China.
052025
092025

Cover Photo: Mihai Andritoiu/Shutterstock Images (skyline); Tatiana Kasyanova/Shutterstock Images (pattern)
Interior Photos: Sergii Figurnyi/Shutterstock Images, 4–5, 8; Shutterstock Images, 9, 12–13, 15, 18 (globe), 27, 28–29, 38, 68–69, 84, 98, 99, 101; Paul B. Moore/Shutterstock Images, 11; Bradley Pietzyk/Shutterstock Images, 14; Sunny Awazuhara-Reed/Alaska Stock/Design Pics Inc./Alamy, 16–17; Red Line Editorial, 18 (United States), 18 (Alaska), 18 (Hawaii); iStockphoto, 21, 24, 37; Jason Patrick Ross/Shutterstock Images, 23; Andrea Izzotti/Shutterstock Images, 31; Belikova Oksana/Shutterstock Images, 32; Sal Galib/Shutterstock Images, 34; Photo by Claudia Domenig/Moment/Getty Images, 35; Richard Maschmeyer/robertharding/Alamy, 40–41; Bettmann/Getty Images, 45; Library of Congress/VCG/Corbis Historical/Getty Images, 48; National Archives/Donaldson Collection/Michael Ochs Archives/Getty Images, 49; AFP/Getty Images, 51; William Philpott/Hulton Archive/Getty Images, 52; Yuen Man Cheung/Alamy, 55; Natural History Library/Alamy, 56–57; Tanveer Anjum Towsif/Shutterstock Images, 58; Jessica Rinaldi/Boston Globe/Getty Images, 61; Ross Marino/Icon and Image/Michael Ochs Archives/Getty Images, 62; Steph Chambers/Getty Images Sport/Getty Images, 65; Esin Deniz/Shutterstock Images, 66; Alex Wong/Getty Images News/Getty Images, 71; Jeff Kowalsky/AFP/Getty Images, 74; US Congress, 76; Michael Nagle/Xinhua/Alamy Live News/Alamy, 78–79; Kean Collection/Archive Photos/Getty Images, 80; Lena Platonova/Shutterstock Images, 85; John Moore/Getty Images News/Getty Images, 86; Marko Aliaksandr/Shutterstock Images, 87; Justin Hamel/Bloomberg/Getty Images, 88–89; Houston Cofield/Bloomberg/Getty Images, 93; Allen J. Schaben/Los Angeles Times/Getty Images, 94; Brent Stirton/Getty Images News/Getty Images, 97

Editor: Marley Richmond
Series Designer: Maggie Villaume

Library of Congress Control Number: 2024948601

PUBLISHER'S CATALOGING-IN-PUBLICATION DATA
Names: Jaskulka, Marie, author.
Title: United States / by Marie Jaskulka
Description: Minneapolis, Minnesota: Abdo Publishing, 2026 | Series: Essential library of countries | Includes online resources and index.
Identifiers: ISBN 9781098297053 (lib. bdg.) | ISBN 9798384919575 (ebook)
Subjects: LCSH: Geography--Juvenile literature. | United States--Civilization--Juvenile literature. | America--Juvenile literature. | United States--History--Juvenile literature.
Classification: DDC 973--dc23

CONTENTS

CHAPTER **ONE**

A TOUR OF THE UNITED STATES

Gracie and her big brother, Latrell, stare at the Statue of Liberty holding her torch up in the air. They had only seen the green statue in books and images online until now. From the oval plane window, Gracie explains the significance of Lady Liberty's spiky crown. She tells her brother it represents a sun spreading light around the world.

For more than a century, people have admired the colossal statue France gifted the United States, and now Gracie and her family are a part of that tradition. As people aboard the plane put away their laptops and books to prepare for landing, Gracie wonders at the magic of finally visiting New York City. She is excited to see what else the bustling city has to offer.

The Statue of Liberty stands on Liberty Island, which people can reach by ferry.

A whir of languages fills Newark Liberty International Airport in New Jersey, one of three major airports that serve New York City. A taxi whisks Gracie, her brother, and their mom through heavy traffic, toll booths, and flashing lights. Vehicles compete for space in the two lanes of traffic slowly entering the Holland Tunnel, a long, dark road completed in 1927 when there wasn't nearly as much traffic. The tunnel runs under the Hudson River and leads to Manhattan, one of the five boroughs that make up New York City.

When the family's taxi emerges from the tunnel, the bright sun blinds Gracie for a few seconds, and then she sees an endless crowd of skyscrapers stretching to the sky in every direction. Pedestrians move between cars, crossing the traffic-filled streets as horns blare. New York City is the most populated city in the United States, and Gracie thinks it is one of the most exciting cities in the world.

AN ULTRA-MODERN SKYLINE

Many of the most iconic buildings in New York City feature an art deco design, with grand, wide-open lobbies, vaulted ceilings, vertical windows, and colorful building materials. This type of architecture was popular globally in the 1920s, when skyscrapers were being constructed across New York City due to its fast-growing population and economy. Preservation societies help ensure that these historic structures can be protected and maintained for future generations to enjoy.

NEW YORK CITY

In Manhattan, Latrell asks to see the view from the top of the Empire State Building, a popular tourist attraction because of its height. The family purchases tickets, waits in line, and takes an elevator ride that seems too short to have lifted them up 86 floors. The view from the top reminds Gracie of being in an airplane, except that wind whips back her hair. People stroll around the observation deck, a level of the building where visitors can get a bird's-eye view from high above the city. Gracie points out the Chrysler Building, and Latrell is the first to spot the Flatiron Building. These are two iconic parts of New York City's skyline. The siblings take turns naming the famous sites they could see from there.

The family walks through Central Park and tries a New York delicacy: a hot dog from a cart parked on the side of the street. The family has only so much time in New York. They are leaving tomorrow on what Gracie's mom calls their Great US Road Trip. They will drive almost 3,000 miles (4,800 km) from New York City on the East Coast to California on the West Coast, stopping to experience some of the most iconic spots in the United States along the way. They will start by heading south toward the White House and the Lincoln Memorial in Washington, DC.

WASHINGTON, DC

Many of the most important national landmarks in Washington, DC, are situated close by one another. They are located around an area of green space called the National Mall, sometimes nicknamed America's Front Yard. Gracie and Latrell run through the grass in between visiting the sites.

Nearly 26 million people visited Washington, DC, in 2023.[1]

The lush green lawn stretches from the US Capitol building to the Lincoln Memorial. The Washington

The Lincoln Memorial honors President Abraham Lincoln for his leadership of the United States.

Monument, a tall white marble pillar, stands between these two structures. It was built to honor the country's first president, George Washington.

Gracie and Latrell admire the large columns that support many of the iconic buildings around them. The Capitol building, where legislators make laws, sits upon a hill slightly higher than everything else. Also surrounding the National Mall are the White House, the Supreme Court, and several important landmarks that honor US veterans, former presidents, changemakers, and leaders.

Gracie's family is lucky enough to be in Washington, DC, on Independence Day. Every year, Americans celebrate the beginning of the United States' independence from Great Britain on July 4. On that day in 1776, a group called the Continental Congress declared the soon-to-be country's autonomy by adopting the Declaration of Independence. On the National Mall, Gracie and Latrell watch fireworks burst with red, white, and blue embers as a band plays patriotic music. Latrell sees the whole scene mirrored in a long reflecting pool on the mall. The celebration inspires immense pride in Gracie. She can't help but think of the historical moments that occurred at this spot.

THE BIRTHPLACE OF COUNTRY MUSIC

In the 1890s, a businessman built an auditorium for people to gather on the banks of the Cumberland River in Nashville, Tennessee. The Union Gospel Tabernacle, eventually called the Ryman Auditorium, was the largest venue south of the Ohio River. It attracted superstars such as Louis Armstrong and Nat King Cole. Southern people who wanted to see or perform live music flocked to Nashville. The music that emerged from the city often reflected life in the South. The Ryman hosted the Grand Ole Opry from 1943 to 1974. This weekly variety show featured up-and-coming country music acts including Johnny Cash and Dolly Parton. Over time, the Ryman helped spread the twangy melodies of country music around the world.

NASHVILLE, TENNESSEE

As the family drives farther away from the East Coast, Gracie observes changes in the landscape. The homes and buildings are farther apart. There is less traffic and more untouched natural space. The family drives through green forests and sees the scenic peaks of the Appalachian Mountains. But soon, the landscape smooths out as the family arrives in the Central Basin of Tennessee.

Nashville, also known as Music City, sits near the Cumberland River in the middle of Tennessee. This town has a rich musical history that goes back to its roots when several musicians and songwriters settled in the region. Gracie and her family tour the

Country Music Hall of Fame. The huge building has giant windows that resemble piano keys. Inside Gracie sees exhibits featuring world-famous musicians' instruments and costumes. Gracie's favorite sights are Elvis Presley's grand piano and his custom gold Cadillac. All too soon, though, it is time for the family to leave Tennessee and continue the road trip.

THE GRAND CANYON

As they cross the United States, Gracie and her family drive up mountains so steep the car slows while climbing them. They also travel along roads so flat and straight they seem to stretch on forever and never bend. But nothing prepares Gracie for the awe she feels when her family stands on a cliff in Grand Canyon National Park in Arizona, watching the sun rise over the Grand Canyon early one morning. Gracie and Latrell enjoy a wide-open sky as the sun illuminates the colorful layers of red, brown, and golden rock that make up the Painted Desert.

Although the temperature is very hot, their July visit allows the family to drive to the highest and least-accessible rim, a flat area where people can view the different features of the canyon. The Grand Canyon has three rims. Tourists can travel to the North Rim, which stands at an elevation of about 8,000 feet (2,400 km), only from May through October. Heavy snowfall makes the roads too dangerous at other times. Because of the difficulty of reaching the North Rim, only about 10 percent of visitors to the Grand Canyon have the chance to visit this highest rim.[2]

Gracie's mom reserved a campsite at this scenic location, so Gracie and Latrell get to work setting up a tent when the family arrives. While there, Gracie and Latrell use binoculars to search

The Colorado River runs through the Grand Canyon. Erosion from this river's flow carved the canyon over millions of years.

The Golden Gate Bridge opened for traffic in 1937. Since then, more than two billion vehicles have crossed the bridge.

for wildlife among the green brush and rocky cliffs. They spot a bighorn sheep with large, curving horns. It strolls confidently across tiny strips of rock. As they leave Grand Canyon National Park the next day, the three stop at an overlook to take a photo in front of the phenomenal sunset.

THE GOLDEN GATE BRIDGE

The road trip stretches through the red dusty deserts of the Southwest, where majestic mesas dot the horizon. Eventually, the landscape shifts back from browns to greens as the family approaches the West Coast. As they arrive in San Francisco, California, Gracie and her mom gasp when they spot a breathtaking bridge in the distance. Two red towers stand as tall as skyscrapers, holding up 1.7 miles (2.7 km) of roadway across the water.[3] Latrell recognizes the bridge from some of his favorite movies. It's the Golden Gate Bridge, which is so famous that it has its own visitors center. The family joins other tourists who enter to learn about how the bridge was designed and built.

"Why is it called the Golden Gate Bridge if it's red?" Latrell asks.

"It was built over the Golden Gate Strait, the body of water that connects the Pacific Ocean to San Francisco Bay," a tour guide explains.

Gracie snaps a group selfie with the iconic bridge in the background to commemorate her trip. She is sure that she will remember her family's Great US Road Trip forever. Gracie and her family take a moment to appreciate the San Francisco skyline as fog envelops the bridge. Gracie wishes the road trip would never end. The journey has opened her eyes to all the sites and landmarks across the United States that she'd like to see. Every road in the United States leads to a new adventure full of surprises and interesting stories.

FROM SEA TO SHINING SEA

From New York City to San Francisco, the United States is full of world-class cities and wild lands. Small towns and unique sights dot the landscape throughout the country. A person could spend a week in each of the 50 states and Washington, DC, and still not see everything the nation has to offer.

Each region has a personality and culture of its own that has been crafted over centuries. These cultures blend American Indian peoples' traditions,

ROADSIDE ATTRACTIONS

One type of US attraction sprung up as a result of Americans' love for road trips. All along the United States' well-traveled highways, people can find weird and fascinating sites called roadside attractions. Many of these places were built to attract motorists after World War II (1939–1945), when highways were being constructed and more people could afford cars. These attractions include the world's largest ball of twine in Cawker City, Kansas, and Nebraska's Carhenge, a re-creation of England's Stonehenge made from classic cars. Roadside attractions still call to a new generation of road trippers who are searching for interesting places to see.

Route 66 is an iconic highway stretching from California to Lake Michigan. It was first advertised as the shortest and most scenic route through the country.

the backgrounds settlers brought with them, and the cultures of immigrants who arrive with big aspirations. Explorers, adventurers, and forward thinkers founded the United States, and the spirit that fueled those quests remains present in the country today.

CHAPTER **TWO**

GEOGRAPHY

The United States is the second-largest country on the North American continent after its northern neighbor, Canada. Covering almost four million square miles (10 million sq km), the United States is the third-largest nation in the world by area.[1] The country includes Alaska and Hawaii, two US states that are separate from the contiguous, or physically connected, US states. The United States is nearly as large as all of Europe, with some US states measuring larger than whole European countries.

Because of its size, the United States has a huge variety of geographic features. The middle of the United States is made of flat plains, while the coasts stretch up into rugged mountains. Some parts of Alaska, such as the North Slope, are covered in tundra, and Hawaii is known for its rainforests. Most of the

Gates of the Arctic National Park protects a swath of geographically diverse land in Alaska.

MAP OF THE UNITED STATES

KEY:

- Capital
- City
- Point of Interest

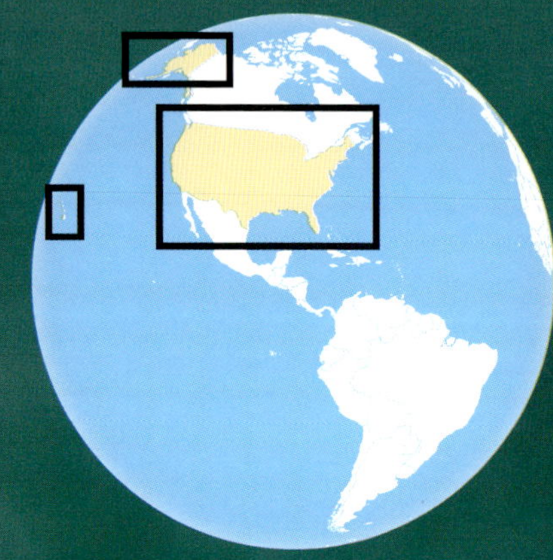

CANADA
Seattle
Mount Rushmore
Mississippi River
Boston
New York City
Philadelphia
Washington, DC
Chesapeake Bay
San Francisco
Arches National Park
Grand Canyon National Park
Las Vegas
Colorado River
Nashville
PACIFIC OCEAN
ATLANTIC OCEAN
Mississippi River
N
W
E
S
New Orleans
MEXICO
GULF OF MEXICO
Everglades National Park

United States has a temperate climate and experiences all four seasons. However, some regions of Alaska are Arctic, and Hawaii and some southern regions of Florida are tropical.

NIAGARA FALLS

Between New York and Canada is a natural wonder known as Niagara Falls. Although it is not the highest waterfall in the world, Niagara is famous because of the amount of water that flows over its crest. Thousands of years ago, a huge glacier slid over the region, carving out land and melting to become the Niagara River. Today, water rushes toward the falls at about 25 miles per hour (40 kmh). Six million cubic feet (170,000 cubic m) of water pour over the falls every minute, slowly eroding rock. The falls have migrated about seven miles (11 km) upstream over the past 12,000 years as rock erodes, and they continue to migrate about one foot (0.3 m) every year.[3]

COASTLINES AND WATERWAYS

Vast coastlines stretch along the eastern and western borders of the United States. Alaska alone has more than 6,600 miles (10,600 km) of rocky coastline along with more than 2,600 islands.[2] Hawaii's islands are known for the tropical beaches along their coasts.

The East Coast borders the Atlantic Ocean. This coastline spans from Maine to Florida and is known as the Eastern Seaboard. Northern East Coast beaches feature cool temperatures, while southern East Coast beaches are warmer for longer periods of the year.

The west side of the country borders the Pacific Ocean. The Coast Ranges are mountains that run parallel to the West Coast from Oregon to California. The coast of California features high sea cliffs and bluffs.

Within its borders, the United States has several major lakes and rivers. The Mississippi River stretches from Minnesota in the north to the Gulf of Mexico in the south, flowing through several major US cities along the way. The Great Lakes are the largest freshwater lakes in the world. They were formed thousands of years ago, when temperatures rose and a glacier that covered the land began to melt and recede. The United States also has several aquifers, which are underground freshwater supplies.

The country's largest estuary, an area where ocean salt water meets fresh water, is the Chesapeake Bay. It is home to more than 3,600 species of animals and plants.[4] Creeks, streams, and rivers throughout New York, Pennsylvania, West Virginia, Maryland, Delaware, Virginia, and Washington, DC, flow into the Chesapeake Bay, which meets the Atlantic Ocean. These waterways provide habitats for aquatic life, along with food, work, and recreational opportunities for people. Many people who live near major waterways have jobs and hobbies that depend on a healthy environment in and around those rivers.

THE NORTHEAST

The Northeast region of the United States is located south of the Canadian border, reaching from Maine down to Pennsylvania and New Jersey. The landscape of the Northeast includes sandy beaches, mountain ranges, and rivers. The Appalachian Mountains start in Canada and stretch down though the Northeast and into Alabama. Several other ranges, such as the Adirondack Mountains, run through the region as well.

The Northeast experiences mild summers and heavy snowfall in winter. The mix of mountains and ocean air creates a humid climate with year-round precipitation. Temperatures in the Northeast occasionally reach above 100 degrees Fahrenheit (38°C) in summer and below zero degrees Fahrenheit (–18°C) in winter. However, the average daily temperatures are more moderate, at about 71 degrees Fahrenheit (22°C) in July and 25 degrees Fahrenheit (–4°C) in January. The Northeast receives about 53 inches (135 cm) of precipitation per year through moderate summer rain and heavy snow, hail, and frozen rain in winter.[5]

PURPLE MOUNTAIN MAJESTIES

In 1893 Katherine Lee Bates, a college professor on a trip out west, rode on a wagon to the top of Pikes Peak in the Rocky Mountains of Colorado. Astounded by the majestic view, Bates said she "felt great joy. All the wonder of the United States seemed displayed there, with the sea-like expanse."[6] Inspired by what she had seen, Bates wrote the poem "America the Beautiful" before returning home. Two years later she published the poem. It grew in popularity, eventually becoming a classic song celebrating the US landscape.

THE MIDWEST

Along the north and middle of the United States, between the Rocky Mountains and the Appalachian Mountains, lie the lakes, plains, and prairies of the Midwest. This region spans from North Dakota in the west to Ohio in the east and south to Kansas. This area of the United States earned the nickname America's Breadbasket because of the many wheat farms there. These farms thrive thanks to fertile soil. Thousands of years ago, glaciers moved across the region, pulverizing rocks and land. The glaciers eventually melted, distributing nutrients into the land.

A high plateau of dry grasslands stretches across the western half of the Midwest. Known as the Great Plains, it spans about 1.1 million square miles (2.8 million sq km), covering almost one-third of the United States.[7] South Dakota's Black Hills and Badlands feature colorful lines that show how layers of rock collected and then partially eroded over millions of years. The northeastern area of the Midwest is the Great Lakes region. Lakes Superior, Michigan, Huron, Erie, and Ontario contain about 90 percent of the fresh water in the United States.[8]

Temperatures vary widely in the Midwest from summer to winter. The region has average highs of about 85 degrees Fahrenheit (29°C) and average lows of 15 degrees Fahrenheit (–9°C).[9] The eastern side of the Midwest receives more precipitation, with levels declining in the west.

The Midwest sometimes experiences extreme weather. The warm, humid wind from the Gulf of Mexico meets the cool, dry Canadian air and causes thunderstorms throughout the year. While many thunderstorms are less than an hour long and consist of moderate wind, rain, lightning, and thunder, they can develop into severe storms.

Tornadoes, which are swirling windstorms, are common in some sections of the Midwest. Part of this region is in an area known as Tornado Alley, which includes North and South Dakota, Nebraska, Iowa,

The granite of the Badlands erodes at a rate of one inch (2.5 cm) per 10,000 years.[10]

Missouri, and Kansas. The atmospheric conditions in this area lead to frequent tornadoes.

THE SOUTH

The South is a region of the United States that stretches from Delaware to Florida on the East Coast and west to Texas and Oklahoma. It has three distinct subregions. These are the temperate forests and coasts in the southeast; the deserts, mesas, and plateaus of the west and southwest; and the warm, rainy, fertile land of the Deep South. The Deep South includes South Carolina, Georgia, Alabama, Mississippi, and Louisiana. Some definitions also include Arkansas and all or part of Florida.

Coastal areas of the South are vulnerable to hurricanes and tropical storms but otherwise enjoy a humid subtropical climate. In summer, high temperatures hit 90 degrees Fahrenheit (32°C). Winter temperatures sink

The Black Hills are known for their forests and mountains. This landscape is home to many plant and animal species.

Swamps, such as Okefenokee Swamp in Georgia, are important geographical features of the South.

down to lows of 32 degrees Fahrenheit (0°C). States farther north experience cooler temperatures than those farther south.[11]

THE WEST

The West is a region that encompasses the western half of the United States from Montana to New Mexico. The West and Southwest are home to deserts, canyons, and plateaus. The Great Basin Desert includes parts of Arizona, Colorado, Idaho, New Mexico, Oregon, Utah, and Wyoming. The landscape is dry with little plant life. Temperatures vary greatly at different elevations but reach 86 degrees Fahrenheit (30°C) in summer and sink to 18 degrees Fahrenheit (–8°C) in winter.[12]

Natural bridges and arches are unique features of the West. Arches National Park in Utah showcases natural arches made of red sandstone worn away by erosion over time. Several mountain ranges also decorate the West. California's Sierra Nevada range boasts granite peaks between 11,000 and 14,000 feet (3,350–4,270 m) above sea level.[13] The Rocky Mountains extend north into Canada and south into New Mexico. They consist of more than 100 smaller mountain ranges.[14]

At the southern border of Canada, the scenic Pacific Northwest is made of rocky coastlines, humid rainforests, snow-capped mountains, and redwood forests. Summers see days up to 90 degrees Fahrenheit (32°C) and near-freezing nights.[15] High elevations get snow even during the summer months. Moving south, the California coastline features a Mediterranean climate of hot, dry summers and mild, rainy winters.

NONCONTIGUOUS US STATES

Alaska borders Canada to the northwest. Alaska's far-north location means its geographic features include glaciers, Arctic tundra, and icy mountain ranges. Temperatures range from average summer highs of about 65 degrees Fahrenheit (18°C) to extreme cold in the winter.[16] Denali, a mountain in Alaska, is the highest peak in North America. Alaska also includes the Aleutian Islands, a chain of islands created by volcanic activity. A few of these volcanoes are still active. The Aleutian Islands separate the Bering Sea and the Pacific Ocean.

Hawaii is the only US state that is an archipelago. It is made entirely of islands. The islands of Hawaii formed from the magma of volcanic eruptions, and some of the state's islands still experience eruptions.

PERMAFROST

Much of the ground in northern Alaska has been frozen for thousands of years. This soil is called permafrost since it has been frozen for at least two years straight. Water cannot penetrate permafrost, so instead of seeping into the ground it pools on the surface and creates lakes. However, Alaska's permafrost has begun to melt due to rising global temperatures. This change is causing problems because the solid ground that supports roads and buildings is growing weak. The Inupiat, a group of Alaska Natives in the North Slope of Alaska, dig ice cellars in the permafrost for cold storage of food, but that tradition is melting away with the permafrost. Lakes are slowly draining, and riverbanks are shifting as this long-frozen land begins to warm.

Although most of Hawaii has year-round tropical temperatures, the high mountain peaks do get some snow. In Hawaii, average summer temperatures are about 80 degrees Fahrenheit (27°C),

Each of Hawaii's islands is the peak of a tall underwater mountain.

and average winter temperatures are about 70 degrees Fahrenheit (21°C). Average yearly rainfall varies widely across different areas of the islands, ranging from 20 to 300 inches (50–760 cm) per year.[17]

CHAPTER **THREE**

PLANTS AND ANIMALS

A variety of biomes can be found across the United States. These are areas classified by the plants and animals that live in them. The nation's diverse biomes allow for a wide range of animals and plants. The natural resources, precipitation, and climate determine the animals and plants that thrive in each area of the country. From the frozen tundra of northern Alaska to the tropical beaches of southern Florida and Hawaii, animals and plants have adapted to thrive in the regions where they live.

Experts estimate that about 34 percent of plant species and 40 percent of animal species in the United States are at risk of extinction.[1] The primary reason so many species are at risk is habitat loss. The United

The bald eagle is the national bird of the United States. These large birds of prey live near bodies of water, where they often hunt.

States is home to more than 300 cities with populations of more than 100,000 people.[2] These urban areas have been developed and altered by humans, who change the environment to improve their own lives. Similarly, agriculture takes up large areas of land. These changes often displace native species and can make them endangered. Human pollution, diseases, and invasive species can also have a negative effect on animal populations.

The Environmental Protection Agency (EPA) and other government and private organizations work to reverse the conditions that threaten species. For instance, the US Fish and Wildlife Service helps people protect or relocate bird nests they find on their property if the nests are at risk of being disturbed. Laws prohibit people from moving the nests and eggs of most songbirds and migratory birds, but trained experts can help homeowners find a solution that protects the animals. US leaders work with environmental scientists to develop recovery plans for natural areas. Together they perform studies, secure funding, create laws, and inform the public to help protect plants and animals.

TEMPERATE FORESTS

Temperate deciduous forests stretch across 26 eastern US states, from Florida to Maine and as far west as Texas.[3] This biome features deciduous trees, such as oaks and maples, whose leaves turn red, orange, yellow, or brown before dropping to the ground. Once bare, the trees turn dormant during the harsh cold of northern winters. Animals in the region, such as deer, squirrels, rabbits, birds, raccoons, chipmunks, frogs, foxes, and songbirds, have adapted to both cold and hot temperatures. Some species hibernate, or spend cold parts of the year in a dormant state. Others, especially birds, migrate during winter. When the air gets colder, fewer insects are available to eat, so birds travel to another location with warmer conditions.

STUDYING DENALI

Reaching an elevation of more than 20,300 feet (6,190 m), the tallest mountain peak in North America is Denali in south-central Alaska.[4] Denali was the first national park in the United States created specifically to protect wildlife. Moose, grizzly bears, caribou, and wolves are some of the large mammals that call the mountain home. Many researchers travel to Denali National Park to study the environment and wildlife. One ongoing study aims to uncover more about the role of wolves in the mountain's ecosystem. Scientists have identified and named many packs on the mountain and continue to study their behavior.

Temperate forests in the Northeast have experienced centuries of land clearing, overhunting, and other alterations. European settlers in the area brought illnesses such as the chestnut blight that damaged native trees that were not resistant to it. The animals that depended on nuts from those trees dwindled. Much of this once-dense temperate forest has been cultivated and developed, but many states have passed laws to preserve large swaths of natural areas.

CONIFEROUS AND BOREAL FORESTS

On the western side of the United States, the largest temperate rainforest in the world stands in the Pacific Northwest. Giant redwood trees in northern

One of the world's largest redwood trees stands in California. It is more than 102 feet (31 m) around at its base.

California rely on the heavy rainfall to reach more than 300 feet (91 m) in height.[5] Various coniferous trees thrive in the region because of their ability to store water in their leaves all year long. Coniferous trees have needlelike or scalelike leaves that stay on all year. Under the huge trees grow mosses, ferns, fungi, lichens, and more. Black bears, owls, elk, salamanders, and beavers are common in this area. The Pacific Northwest provides the perfect environment for salmon to reproduce in cold mountain streams that flow down into the Pacific Ocean. The orcas in the Pacific eat some of the salmon.

Boreal forests take up a small percentage of the United States' land, but they are extraordinarily important. Forming a circle around the North Pole, boreal forests cover most of Alaska and some of the northernmost US states. Coniferous trees including spruce, fir, and pine grow in this area along with other plants well suited to cold climates, such as fireweed. Boreal forests store large amounts of carbon in the soil and trees, which helps regulate Earth's climate. Brown and black bears, moose, wolves, ravens, and eagles live in boreal forests and have adapted to the long, harsh winters of this biome.

RAINFORESTS AND TROPICAL FORESTS

Hawaii's 2,600 square miles (6,700 sq km) of tropical rainforests are home to a huge variety of animals and plants.[6] Hawaii has several plants that can't be found anywhere else in the world. One is the ʻōhiʻa lehua, a plant with colorful flowers often included in Hawaiian lei, flower necklaces that are traditional gifts of friendship in the islands. The nēnē is a small striped goose unique to Hawaii. It has long legs and very little webbing on its toes, adaptations to living much of its life on land. Although the nēnē migrates, it doesn't need to leave Hawaii. Instead the nēnē migrates from sea level to much higher elevations as conditions change.

The southeastern tip of the United States is also home to tropical forests, sometimes called hammocks, that look similar to the landscape of a Caribbean island. These forests are one of the few places where the elusive ghost orchid grows. The red-barked gumbo limbo tree, sometimes called the tourist tree because its bark resembles sunburned skin, is also common in the humid brush. Flocks of long-legged pink flamingos can be seen wading in shallow water, dipping their black-tipped beaks to scoop up shrimp.

The largest bald eagle's nest ever found was 9.5 feet (2.9 m) across, was 20 feet (6 m) deep, and weighed more than 4,000 pounds (1,800 kg).[7]

TUNDRA, MOUNTAINS, AND WETLANDS

Northern Alaska is an inhospitable region called a tundra, but many animals thrive in this cold, harsh environment where there is very little vegetation. Mosses, lichens, shrubs, and wildflowers are common plants there. Caribou, Arctic foxes, snowy owls, musk oxen, and polar bears live in the tundra as well. Over the last 50 years, climate change and other factors have affected the area. Permafrost, which is ground that has been frozen solid for at least two years, has begun to melt. This has forced many animals to move farther north where temperatures are cooler.

The United States is home to several mountain ranges, including the Rocky Mountains, Sierra Nevada, Appalachian Mountains, and Alaska Range. Because of their high elevations, mountains are home to plants and animals adapted to large temperature changes in short periods of time and differences in air pressure. Lupine and alpine forget-me-not wildflowers decorate the rocky landscapes. Goats and bighorn sheep balance on high, narrow cliffs. Their split hooves and rough hoof skin make them experts at balance.

THE WORLD'S OLDEST LIVING TREE

A Great Basin bristlecone pine in eastern California is widely considered the oldest living tree on Earth. Scientists nicknamed the tree Methuselah, and its exact location is kept secret for its own protection. This almost 5,000-year-old tree is important not just for its beauty and longevity but for what it shows about the perseverance of nature. A tree that can survive in the Great Basin Desert's harsh, unforgiving conditions proves the resilience and strength of nature.

Florida is home to the American flamingo, also called the Caribbean flamingo. These birds stand about five feet (1.5 m) tall and live along the coast.

Wetlands are spread throughout the southeastern United States and Gulf Coast. The Everglades make up a large area of subtropical wetlands in southern Florida. Alligators, frogs, snakes, water skinks, herons, duckweed, shrimp, and crawfish call the swampland and marshes of the Everglades home. Amphibians, which usually lay their eggs in water but live most of their lives on land, thrive in the shallow waters and moist lands of this biome. Everglades National Park protects many plant and animal species in this region.

DRY BIOMES

Grasses and sagebrush dominate the landscape of the central United States in the Great Plains. Bison, coyotes, prairie dogs, and pronghorn are some of the most common animals in this region. Millions of bison, the largest land mammal in North America, once roamed the Great Plains, keeping themselves and the land healthy by grazing on the grasses. European settlers who arrived in the region in the 1800s hunted bison to near extinction. Today, only 31,000 wild bison remain.[8]

The southwestern and western United States are home to plants and animals that have adapted

WHEN BEARS ROAMED CALIFORNIA

California's state flag features its official state animal, the California grizzly bear. These wild beasts weighed approximately 1,000 pounds (450 kg) and measured up to eight feet (2.4 m) in height when standing on their hind legs.[9] Long before humans arrived in California, they roamed the region freely. Early California settlers created the Bear Flag to symbolize their independence and strength. By the 1920s, California grizzlies had become extinct as a result of humans settling in California and overhunting. But the flag remains, making California the only state flag featuring an extinct animal.

Joshua trees are known for their twisted shapes, spiky trunks, and tufts of leaves. They provide shelter and food to birds and reptiles.

to hot, bright, dry conditions. Saguaro cacti, Joshua trees, prickly pear cacti, and creosote bushes conserve water. Saguaro cacti have long, wide-spreading, shallow roots and waxy skin that help soak up water and prevent moisture loss. Rattlesnakes, Gila monsters, desert tortoises, turkey

Black-tailed jackrabbits use their large ears to regulate their body temperature.

vultures, and scorpions are some common wildlife in US deserts. Many stay underground or sleep during the hot day and get water through food.

Chaparral thrives in the hot, dry summers and mild winters of central and southern California. This type of landscape is dominated by coniferous shrubs with stiff, leathery leaves that store water well. Lizards, spotted owls, black-tailed jackrabbits, and coyotes have adapted to the dry climate, droughts, and wildfires. The area gets frequent wildfires, and certain species of sparrows live in burned chamise trees. A few years after a fire comes through, birds will settle in the area.

THIS LAND IS YOUR LAND

The United States forms a vast tapestry of different landscapes because the country is so large. However, urban areas continue to expand through suburban sprawl and the consistent development of rural spaces. Growing populations of humans are producing pollution that further harms natural spaces and wildlife. Overhunting has historically eliminated some species to the point of extinction.

US national parks recorded more than 300 million visits in 2023.[11]

Human development has altered the landscape, but forward thinkers have long been working to preserve nature by making laws to protect it. Legislation protects natural resources and promotes the reclamation of places that have been damaged by human development. There are 433 national parks, seashores, monuments, and other federally protected areas across the 50 states, the District of Columbia, and US territories.[10] The US government protects and maintains these locations so that many more people can enjoy the natural beauty of the United States for generations to come. Protected areas can even reverse human damage by serving as safe habitats for endangered wildlife.

CHAPTER **FOUR**

HISTORY

Scientists hypothesize that the first humans arrived in North America between 25,000 and 16,000 years ago.[1] The millions of Indigenous people who lived in North America long before Europeans arrived on the continent had diverse cultures. Cultures and groups of nations including the Ancestral Puebloans in the southwest, Mississippians in the southeast, and the Iroquois Confederacy in the northeast all had their own religions, philosophies, languages, political systems, and trade.

It is difficult to know the number of distinct Indigenous nations that existed in North America before European colonization. American Indian peoples spoke between 300 and 500 languages.[2] Experts use this number to estimate the number of cultural groups in the region.

Petroglyphs, or rock art, provide one record of ancient peoples and cultures in the United States. The Procession Panel is a well-known petroglyph created by the Ancestral Puebloans between 500 and 750 CE.

Christopher Columbus was an Italian explorer whose 1492 voyage from Europe to North America paved the way for mass European settlement of the continent. Early European settlers saw vast resources in the Americas that they wanted to seize, including farmland and deposits of gold. European exploration of North America continued through the 1600s as the Spanish ventured into the South and Southwest. French settlers moved into the Mississippi River Valley from the north. English people landed and built communities on the Atlantic Coast.

Explorers viewed North America as an unclaimed, valuable New World, and they saw American Indians as uncivilized people who didn't own or have a claim to the land where they lived. Throughout the 1500s and 1600s, European settlers battled and killed American Indians in an effort to take over and colonize the land that would become the United States. Although American Indian people fought back, sometimes successfully, Europeans had brought more powerful weapons and also new diseases that wiped out entire American Indian populations and weakened their forces.

TECUMSEH, CELESTIAL PANTHER LYING IN WAIT

A shooting star fell on the night Tecumseh, a Shawnee warrior and speaker, was born in 1768. This is how he earned his name, which means "Celestial Panther Lying in Wait." Tecumseh believed that European settlers would never be satisfied until they had eradicated all American Indian nations. Tecumseh envisioned uniting American Indian peoples across the continent who once had warred with each other in order to defeat the Europeans. Tecumseh orchestrated an alliance with British soldiers. While he wasn't successful in defeating the colonists, he is still celebrated as a champion of American Indian rights.

Great Britain sent a steady stream of people and money to North America to build settlements called colonies. These colonies would benefit Britain economically through the trade of natural resources. In the early 1600s, Jamestown became the first British colony in North America. Soon, European settlers formed 12 more colonies along and near the East Coast. Each colony made its own government, but Britain held the ultimate power. Colonists began to resent having to pay high taxes to the British king without being allowed any representation in the British government.

In 1772 colonial leaders began to meet to secretly discuss their ideas about declaring independence from Great Britain. Colonial leaders formed the Continental Congress and met for a series of meetings to plan their next actions. In 1775 fighting began in Massachusetts, launching the American Revolution (1775–1783). While many colonists sided with Britain, others flocked to join the Continental Army, holding their own against British forces. The Continental Congress endorsed the Declaration of Independence, a summary of the colonists' reasons for seeking freedom, on July 4, 1776, but fighting continued. France, Spain, and the Netherlands backed the colonists, helping the Americans win their independence officially in 1783.

SLAVERY

Dutch colonists brought the first enslaved African people to North America in the early 1600s to work on farms. This was the beginning of the slave trade in the United States, during which millions of Africans were brought to the United States and sold. Nearly two million people died on the journey before the international slave trade was banned in the United States in 1808.[3]

However, the domestic slave trade continued after 1808 as slave owners bought and sold enslaved people and their descendants. Enslaved people were forced to work under inhumane conditions for no pay, and they had no legal or civil rights. They worked in the homes of white slavers and on large farms, especially on plantations that grew labor-intensive crops such as tobacco, sugar, and cotton in the South.

US EXPANSION

During the early 1800s, the United States continued to grow, expanding beyond the original 13 states born from the colonies. In 1803 the US government purchased a large area of land from France. This transaction was called the Louisiana Purchase, and it doubled the size of the United States. The land purchased became eight states and portions of five more.[4]

As Americans began to settle west of the original 13 states, conflict arose with the American Indian peoples who lived there. The US government acquired some land east of the Mississippi River through treaties with American Indian peoples including the Cherokee, Chickasaw, and Creek nations. But Americans wanted to settle farther west as well. In 1830 the US Congress passed the Indian Removal Act, which required American Indians east of the Mississippi to leave their land. This legislation led to the Trail of Tears, a period during which 100,000 American Indians were forced to relocate hundreds of miles away. About 15,000 of those people died on the journey.[5]

The US government continued to claim new lands, now turning its attention to the southwest. During the Mexican-American War (1846–1848), US forces succeeded against Mexican forces.

Explorers Meriwether Lewis and William Clark led an exploration to chart the land of the Louisiana Purchase. Sacagawea, *pointing*, was a Shoshone Indian woman who helped guide their voyage.

In 1848 the US government signed a treaty with Mexico that handed over Mexican land. This land would eventually make up six new states and part of a seventh, from California to Texas.[6]

THE CIVIL WAR

In addition to its physical growth, the United States saw immense economic growth in the 1800s, most of which wouldn't have been possible without the labor of enslaved people. At the same time, the abolitionist movement grew, calling for the end of all slavery in the United States. Tensions rose between Northern states, which did not economically rely on slavery, and Southern states, which did. These tensions increased as new states were added to the union. People began to wonder whether it was possible to have a single government over such a large area of land with conflicting interests.

Seven US states left the United States between 1860 and 1861, forming the Confederate States of America. These states fought with the remaining US states, called the Union, in the American Civil War (1861–1865). This conflict focused on national versus state power and its implications in the

THE WOMEN OF THE CIVIL WAR

At the time of the Civil War, only men were allowed to enlist in the military, but many women who wanted to join didn't let that stop them. Most soldiers stayed fully dressed at all times, even while sleeping, so women in baggy clothes could pass as men enlisting to fight. Researchers estimate that about 1,000 women disguised themselves and fought in the Civil War.[7] Today some women dress up like men and join Civil War reenactments to pay tribute to those brave female Civil War soldiers.

continuation of slavery. It determined how the United States would move forward—as a loose confederation of sovereign states or a strong union under one federal government.

The Union's victory solidified the national government and led to the end of slavery in the United States. It was followed by a period called Reconstruction. During this time, millions of people were freed from slavery, and the US government was tested as some people continued to resist change. Many Black people were denied their new rights, especially in Southern states, and had to launch legal battles to uphold their freedoms.

WORLD WARS AND THE GREAT DEPRESSION

The Industrial Revolution in the late 1800s and early 1900s brought huge economic growth to the United States, especially in industries such as steel and oil. An expanded railroad system connected the nation and brought regions of the United States that were less populated into the national economy. Many Americans became wealthy through these new ventures, but the projects required large amounts of general laborers. Immigrants and people in rural areas flocked to urban areas, forming the working class, who were often treated unfairly.

Leaders among the working class began pushing for improved working conditions and better wages. They became known as progressives, alongside others who worked to make life better by pointing out government corruption, inequality, and other problems. Progressives petitioned for laws that would protect the rights of the most vulnerable people in society. For example, progressives worked to secure women's right to vote.

During the Great Depression, some churches and charities ran soup kitchens that provided free meals to people who could not afford enough food.

In 1917 the United States joined World War I (1914–1918) on the side of the Allies, who fought the Central Powers led by Germany. One of the war's central issues was the expansion of European empires, but an attack killing US citizens brought the United States out of its position of neutrality. More than one million US military members joined in the conflict before the Allies won.[8]

The United States' economic rise through the 1920s fell off a cliff on October 29, 1929, on a day that came to be known as Black Tuesday. Stock rates fell dramatically, and many people lost the savings they had invested in the stock market. This crash was the start of a period of global economic hardship called the Great Depression. It would take about a decade for the US economy to recover from this crash. During those ten years, global tensions rose in part due to the economic stress of the Great Depression.

World War II (1939–1945) began in Europe in 1939. The Allies, led by the United Kingdom and the Soviet Union, fought against the extreme nationalist governments of the Axis powers, including Germany, Italy, and Japan. The United States remained neutral in this conflict until Japan attacked Pearl Harbor, a US military base in the Pacific, in 1941.

This attack on US soil motivated the US government to enter the conflict by declaring war against Japan. Germany and Italy declared war against the United States soon after. Millions of

AN ICON FOR STRONG WOMEN

Rosie the Riveter, a figure who appeared on posters during World War II, is a symbol of female strength in pop culture. The war required many men to travel abroad to fight. This resulted in a shakeup of gender norms as women entered the workplace to fill jobs left behind by soldiers, including jobs men traditionally held. Although Rosie the Riveter was a subject of songs and art, she was not a real person. She was a symbol of the way women contributed to the war effort. The most famous image of Rosie shows her wearing a red bandana over her hair and rolling up her sleeves under the words "We can do it!"

Almost 25 percent of the US workforce was unemployed at the height of the Great Depression.[9]

Americans joined the military. Many others took war-related jobs in fast-growing war industries, all of which caused an economic boom that helped the US economy return to a state of prosperity. The Allies won the war in 1945.

THE COLD WAR AND THE VIETNAM WAR

Tensions between the Soviet Union and the United States, once allies, rose as the two nations vied for power in the postwar world. The US government aimed to prevent the spread of communism, which the Soviet Union championed. The ensuing Cold War (1947–1991) marked a period of global fear and uncertainty.

Although there was no direct armed conflict between the United States and the Soviet Union, the Cold War led in part to US involvement in the Vietnam War (1954–1975). The United States supported South Vietnam in its fight against communist North Vietnam, backed by the Soviet Union. The US military first deployed combat troops to Vietnam in 1965.

As the conflict progressed, US conscription rates rose and progress in the war remained unclear. An anti-war movement began in colleges and universities, and soon a significant proportion of Americans opposed the war. By 1973 the US government negotiated US withdrawal from the conflict. Two years later, the war ended as South Vietnam fell to the North. In total

Protests were an important part of the movement against US involvement in the Vietnam War. Activists gathered around the nation, especially on college campuses and in Washington, DC, throughout the conflict.

approximately 58,000 US servicemembers died alongside about two million Vietnamese civilians and approximately 1.3 million Vietnamese soldiers and militia members.[10]

CIVIL RIGHTS AND ACTIVISM

After World War II, the US economy had continued to grow, but some groups were left out of the United States' success. Racial segregation kept Black Americans excluded from the opportunities

ROSA PARKS

Rosa Parks was born in Tuskegee, Alabama, in 1913. Parks grew up in the South while it was segregated, and she and her family experienced racism throughout her childhood. For example, Parks and other Black children had to attend schools separate from their white peers. Teachers at schools for Black children had fewer resources. In 1943 Parks joined the National Association for the Advancement of Colored People (NAACP), an organization pushing for desegregation and equal rights for Black people.

On December 1, 1955, Parks was riding a bus in Montgomery, Alabama. The driver asked her to give her seat to a white passenger. But Parks refused to move. She was arrested for this choice.

Building off several years of activist efforts, Parks's arrest began a wave of protests called the Montgomery Bus Boycott. For more than a year, Black people refused to ride Montgomery buses, and people around the nation took similar actions against segregation. This movement led to the desegregation of public transportation around the country. Parks was one of many people fighting segregation. She had a lasting impact on US laws and history.

Rosa Parks remained an activist until her death in 2005.

that many white Americans enjoyed. US laws enforced the segregation of white and Black people in public spaces and withheld civil and legal rights for many people.

During the civil rights movement in the 1960s, leaders such as Martin Luther King Jr. and Rosa Parks led marches, staged sit-ins, organized boycotts, and filed lawsuits to obtain equal rights and opportunities for Black people. One major success of this period was the Civil Rights Act of 1964, a law that made it illegal to discriminate against people based on their race, color, religion, sex, or national origin.

THE ROAD TO A NEW MILLENNIUM

Amid political turmoil at home and abroad, the United States also entered a period of technological advancement. The space race was yet another avenue for the United States to prove its superiority to the Soviet Union. Rocket technology could be used not only for scientific discovery but also for weapons. The two nations strove to be the first to land astronauts on the moon. The United States succeeded in 1969, when the Apollo 11 mission touched down on the moon's surface.

The 1970s saw the founding of Microsoft, a pioneering US software company. The internet came online in 1983. In 1989 the World Wide Web began to connect users across the globe, and US companies made it easier than ever to access and navigate the internet. A pop culture boom in the 1990s saw the rise of musical genres such as grunge and hip-hop, the premiere of globally popular TV shows such as *Friends*, and the release of blockbuster films such as *Titanic*.

By the early 1990s, the Soviet Union's power had begun to fade. The nation officially collapsed in 1991, bringing the Cold War to an end. By the turn of the millennium, the United States had situated itself as the world's foremost political and cultural superpower.

GLOBAL CHALLENGES

On September 11, 2001, terrorists linked to the Islamist extremist group al-Qaeda took over four commercial airliners in midair. Terrorists flew two of the planes into the World Trade Center skyscrapers in New York City and one into the Pentagon, the headquarters of the US military in Arlington, Virginia. A fourth plane crashed in a field in Pennsylvania after passengers fought back in an attempt to stop the hijackers. Nearly 3,000 people were killed in the terrorist attack.[11]

Al-Qaeda's attack was an attempt to weaken the US government and end Western influence in the Middle East. This aim was unsuccessful, as the US government responded by increasing its presence in the region and deploying troops to Afghanistan, where government officials believed al-Qaeda was being sheltered by the Taliban, the group that controlled Afghanistan. However, the attack did change life in the United States. Security measures were put in place through the creation of a government organization called the Department of Homeland Security. These measures included the creation of the Transportation Security Administration (TSA), which oversees security measures at airports to prevent similar attacks from happening.

Decades later, new global threats emerged. In March 2020, the World Health Organization announced that the respiratory disease COVID-19 had become a global pandemic. Soon after,

The 9/11 Memorial has two pools located where the World Trade Center's twin towers once stood.

governments across the United States began to shut down schools and nonessential businesses. More than one million Americans died from COVID-19 between 2019 and 2024.[12] The pandemic led to social and economic disruptions that Americans would be dealing with for years to come. Although many aspects of daily life in the United States returned to their pre-pandemic states by 2023, effects of the pandemic, along with COVID-19 itself, are still present throughout the country.

CHAPTER **FIVE**

PEOPLE AND CULTURE

The United States was once described as a shining city on a hill, a symbol of hope and opportunity that draws people to it with the promise of a better life. That vision of a fair shot for anyone who is willing to work for it is alive and well today in people all over the world. In 2022 about 2.6 million people legally immigrated to the United States.[1] The main reasons people come to the United States are to obtain work or education, to reunite with family, or to seek safety.

DEMOGRAPHICS

Today, the United States is home to more than 340 million people.[2] About 14 percent of the population

Immigrants may apply for US citizenship. If their applications are approved, they take the Oath of Allegiance at a naturalization ceremony and become US citizens.

was born outside of the country.[3] The foreign-born population of the United States includes both people who have and have not completed the United States' legal immigration process.

With a constant influx of influences from all over the globe, the United States is an always-fluctuating tapestry of heritage, race, and socioeconomic classes. The most common ethnic groups are white at 61.6 percent, Black at 12.4 percent, Asian at 6 percent, Indigenous and Alaska Native at 1.1 percent, Native Hawaiian and Other Pacific Islander at 0.2 percent, other ethnicities at 8.4 percent, and two or more races at 10.2 percent. Almost 19 percent of the population is Hispanic, a designation that intersects with several races and ethnicities.[4] As is the case in other nations, US culture is not singular. Thousands of regional lifestyles contribute to the whole picture.

LIFE ON THE BAYOU

Sections of the US Gulf Coast, sometimes called bayou country, have a distinct language, diet, and way of life. With access to the Mississippi and Missouri River system, the area became a popular port where French, African, and American Indian cultures merged in the 1600s and 1700s. Cajun and Creole people trace their roots back to these people who made their homes in the region. Bayous, the swampy waterways that flow through the region, are abundant. Seafood is a common ingredient in Cajun and Creole recipes such as jambalaya.

LANGUAGE AND RELIGION

The United States has no official language, but English is the most common, with 78 percent of Americans speaking only English.[5] States are allowed, but not mandated, to designate an official

AMERICAN INDIAN LANGUAGES

Before Europeans arrived in North America, Indigenous languages flourished. About 300 languages were spoken across North America, although some American Indian peoples didn't use writing systems.[10] Instead they had strong oral traditions, meaning they passed down ideas, history, and stories through the spoken word. As Europeans displaced American Indian peoples, colonization drove many languages to extinction as fewer living people spoke them. Many American Indian children were sent to boarding schools where they were forbidden from speaking in languages other than English. More than 60 Indigenous languages are now extinct, and more than 70 are in danger of being lost.[11]

language, and 32 of the 50 states have made theirs English.[6] Hawaiian is an official language in the state of Hawaii, and 20 Alaskan Native languages are official in Alaska.[7]

People in the United States speak about 350 different languages. Almost one-fifth of people in the United States speak a language other than English at home.[8] Some may also speak English outside the home. The most widely used languages other than English are Spanish, Chinese (Mandarin and other varieties), Tagalog, Vietnamese, and Arabic.

The United States is also diverse when it comes to religion, with Americans practicing a variety of faiths. Nearly 70 percent of Americans have Christian-based faiths, with Protestantism and Catholicism being the most-practiced branches. More than 20 percent of Americans consider themselves unaffiliated with any religion. People of Jewish, Muslim, and Buddhist faiths, along with others, make up less than 6 percent of the population.[9] People in the United States may also choose to convert to a new religion for reasons such as marriage or a change in views.

HOLIDAYS

Many holidays observed in the United States have religious ties, although people of many religions often join in celebrations. Christians may celebrate Christmas on December 25, honoring the birth of Jesus Christ, who they believe is the son of God. Some Christians attend mass at midnight on Christmas Eve, December 24, to honor the hour Jesus was born. Muslims may observe Ramadan, a holy month during which they practice self-restraint. One Ramadan tradition is fasting between dawn and dusk. Eid al-Fitr marks the end of Ramadan and is often an occasion for family gatherings.

Jews may celebrate Hanukkah, an eight-day holiday typically falling in December. Hanukkah commemorates the Jewish reclamation of the Holy Temple in Jerusalem in the 100s BCE. Jews often light one candle on a menorah for each night of Hanukkah. Hindu people may celebrate Holi, the Festival of Colors, which often falls in March. This joyful festival is rooted in Hindu mythology and celebrates good winning out over evil.

Many other popular celebrations have no religious ties. Memorial Day honors fallen service members in the US military and is celebrated on the last Monday in May. Labor Day celebrates the achievements of US workers on the first Monday in September.

On Thanksgiving, many families gather to eat a large meal and share gratitude. This holiday falls on the fourth Thursday in November. Indigenous Peoples' Day became a national holiday in 2021 as an opportunity to recognize and celebrate American Indians and their contributions to the nation, both past and present. It falls on the second Monday in October.

American Indians may celebrate Indigenous Peoples' Day by sharing their culture through dance. The eastern blanket dance is performed by some Mashpee Wampanoag Tribe members.

Aretha Franklin is known as the Queen of Soul. Her gospel-inspired musical career began in the 1950s and has inspired many musicians since then.

ENTERTAINMENT AND THE ARTS

Americans have a wide variety of drama, music, and architectural arts to enjoy, partly because the government funds artists and organizations that support creative work. The largest single funder of the arts across the United States is the National Endowment for the Arts. This federal agency gives out grants for artists to complete and share their work.

Musical productions and theatrical plays have been staged in New York City since the mid-1700s, and Broadway has become a global symbol of US theater. This long strip of theaters in Manhattan was one of the first streets in the United States to have electric lights, earning it the nickname the Great White Way. Dozens of new productions debut in Broadway theaters. Millions of people watch Broadway performances every year. In 1985 approximately 6.5 million tickets were sold. By 2024 that number reached more than 12 million.[12]

An industry on the other side of the United States exports some of the most famous films, movies, and television shows in the world. Hollywood, California, is home to a collection of TV and film studios that pride themselves on creating compelling dramas and hilarious comedies. Although many of the most popular US movies focus on superheroes, smaller independent filmmakers produce experimental, artistic films that are well-received by audiences around the country.

STORYTELLING TRADITIONS

Historically, many aspects of US language, food, and music were heavily influenced by the traditions enslaved people brought from their homelands. One example is storytelling. Enslaved people told their children Anansi stories, folktales in which a clever spider outsmarts bigger animals. The Ashanti people in Ghana originated these stories, and they grew into Brer Rabbit stories in the United States. In these stories, an intelligent rabbit outsmarts larger animals.

Music has always played a strong role in US culture. Jazz, blues, rock 'n' roll, hip-hop, country, and electronic dance music (EDM) are all genres that emerged from life in the United States. Many genres of music evolved from the people, influences, and history of the country, especially Black people. Some genres were shaped by immigrants as well.

In the late 1800s, blues emerged after the Civil War as the country adapted to the end of slavery. Influenced by spiritual music, work songs, and popular music of the time, blues expressed the emotions of long-oppressed Black Americans. A century later, hip-hop emerged from urban centers where young people expressed the struggles of living in post-segregation society over a backdrop of sounds made by new technology. Performers scratched records, programmed drum machines, and sampled other people's music to make their own.

Many US visual artists left a mark on the world. One was John Singleton Copley, who re-created war scenes during the 1700s and early 1800s. Modernist Georgia O'Keeffe is known for her bright, colorful, feminine blooms. She became an American icon during the 1900s.

US artwork is as diverse as its people. Jackson Pollock conveyed this through abstract expressionist work, believing that the way paint dripped and moved on a canvas was an art form of its own. Andy Warhol blended commercial images with fine art to popularize a genre called pop art. Norman Rockwell created realistic but idealized images of US family life in a style called photorealism, while Jean-Michel Basquiat brought attention to race and identity tension through his graffiti-inspired works. Contemporary artists reflect the ideas and struggles present in their communities and in society.

The history of the United States is also reflected in the country's architecture. Many of the buildings in Washington, DC, were designed in a neoclassical style to honor the Greek and Roman governments that inspired the nation's founders. During the extraordinary economic prosperity of the 1920s, soaring skyscrapers stretched to the clouds of New York City, reflecting how unstoppable Americans felt at the time. Beginning in the early 1900s, Frank Lloyd Wright introduced an organic kind of architecture that blended in with nature rather than disrupting it. For instance, he built a home full of large windows and without roof gutters so people inside could view the icicles that formed.

The Super Bowl is one of the most popular sporting events in the United States. This final faceoff between two National Football League teams draws many millions of viewers every year.

Today's architecture often reflects ideas of equity for all. Many structures are designed so that everyone, no matter their size or physical abilities, can enjoy the space. This might mean including windows at various heights so all people get a chance to see the view.

SPORTS AND FOOD

In the United States, many cities have professional sports teams filled with world-famous athletes. There are more than 150 professional sports leagues, such as the Women's National Basketball Association and Major League Soccer.[13] Baseball, basketball, American football, and ice hockey are some of the most popular sports in the country. More than half of American children six to 17 years old play sports on a team or take sporting lessons.[14]

Early British settlers in the United States learned how to make apple pie from Dutch immigrants.

Diversity abounds in the vast variety of food available to Americans. Burgers, hot dogs, and apple pie are all considered quintessential US foods, but many regions have their own specialties that emerged from the cultural influences and natural resources in each area. In the Southwest, Tex-Mex blends traditional Mexican cooking techniques with ingredients available in Texas to create US versions of Mexican dishes. Southern cuisine is characterized not just by bold flavors and hearty helpings but also by the South's complex history. Tamales are popular in the Mississippi delta because Mexican people migrated there to work in the early 1900s. Soul food came from Black Southerners, but its roots can be further traced back to Africa. Africans brought many cooking traditions to the United States during the days of slavery, fusing them with American Indian and European styles.

The United States has a negative reputation when it comes to the health and nutritional value of its food. The Standard American Diet, a common eating pattern in the United States, contains a lot of added salt, fat, and processed sugar. The US government has made efforts to bring awareness to the benefits of shifting to a more nutritious diet. For instance, the US Department of Agriculture regularly creates recommended dietary guidelines and public campaigns to teach people about the benefits of eating more whole foods such as fruits and vegetables.

On average, Americans consume about 17 teaspoons (71 g) of added sugar a day, which equates to about 60 pounds (26 kg) a year.[15]

CHAPTER **SIX**

POLITICS

The people who created the US government wanted to establish a system influenced by philosophers who wrote about how government should function. One example is John Locke, a British philosopher and writer who suggested that rulers should have power only over people who willfully give it to them. This idea influenced the democratic nature of the US government. Locke also championed the idea of separation of church and state, the belief that the government should not be tied to a particular religion. This separation is another pillar of the US government.

The founding fathers created the US Constitution as the central guiding document for the new US government. The US Constitution defines how the national government should operate, and all US laws

The US Capitol building in Washington, DC, is home to the US Congress. Congressmembers' offices are also located in the Capitol.

must honor its protections. It reflects the founders' idea that a nation's people, not an elite group of leaders, should hold the ultimate power in government. The power of the government should in turn be limited so it cannot oppress the people.

Most of all, the founders wanted individuals to be able to live their lives the way they wanted without other people telling them what to believe and how to live. The founding fathers granted these rights to only a limited part of society, however, leaving out women, minorities, and people who didn't own land. Subsequent generations have worked to expand these freedoms in the United States.

BRANCHES OF GOVERNMENT

The United States is a constitutional federal republic, meaning that national and state governments share power. The headquarters of national government is located in the District of Columbia, or Washington, DC. In 1790 the US Congress set aside 100 square miles (260 sq km) of land to serve as the nation's capital.[1] The federal government oversees the 50 individual self-governing states. According to the Constitution, powers not given to the federal government are reserved for the states. These include running schools and administering elections. Just as Washington, DC, is the capital of the country, every state has a capital city where its state government is based. Counties, cities, and towns in each state also have their own governments.

About 156.3 million people voted in the 2024 US presidential election.[2]

In a republic, people elect leaders to represent them in government. Leaders have a responsibility to advocate for the needs and values of their constituents. Constituents are the people a leader represents.

The federal and state governments each have executive, legislative, and judicial branches. The executive branch enforces laws. In the national government, this branch is led by the president. Donald Trump took office as the nation's forty-seventh president in 2025. The executive branch also includes the president's advisers and cabinet. The cabinet includes the vice president and leaders of various departments that oversee aspects of the government. Cabinet members include the secretary of defense, the secretary of the treasury, and the head of the EPA, among others.

Congress, the legislative branch, is made of the House of Representatives and the Senate.

Ketanji Brown Jackson was sworn in as a Supreme Court justice on June 30, 2022, becoming the first Black woman to serve in the role.

Congress makes laws, declares war, and controls spending. There are 100 members of the US Senate, with two senators from each state, and 435 members of the House of Representatives. Seats in the House are allocated by state population, with larger states having more members. Each state has at least one representative. The most populated state, California, has 52.

The judicial branch is made of the US Supreme Court and the federal court system. These courts listen to arguments when people disagree with a law, and then justices use their deep knowledge of the Constitution to decide who is correct. If someone questions a law, they can challenge the law in the judicial branch. Many smaller courts throughout the country make up the state court system.

By separating powers, the founders aimed to create a system of checks and balances so the government could regulate itself. The president can veto legislation passed by Congress. Congress can reject presidential nominees for positions of power. Supreme Court justices can overturn laws they deem unconstitutional. Because all matters must be agreed on and discussed between all three branches, it is difficult for any one branch to become too powerful.

The president, vice president, and members of Congress are all elected. Once candidates decide to run for office, they publicize their beliefs through campaigns and discuss their approaches to government problems in debates. Every eligible American who is at least 18 years old may vote.

Presidential elections occur every four years in the United States. These elections use a special system called the Electoral College. Each state has a designated number of votes in the Electoral

College depending on its population. These votes are cast by electors, who usually base their vote on the popular vote in their state.

Federal judges are nominated by the president and confirmed by Congress. Congress may reject a nominee, although this is not common. Judges serve a life term, meaning they may hold their position until their death or chosen retirement.

THE DONKEY AND THE ELEPHANT

Political cartoons date back to the United States' beginnings, when upset colonists published their grievances. During Andrew Jackson's 1828 presidential campaign, Jackson embraced the insults hurled by his opponents and took on the donkey as a symbol of his campaign. To him, the donkey represented tenacity. Artists started using donkeys to represent Democratic politicians. Abraham Lincoln used an elephant in a campaign poster during the Civil War when "seeing the elephant" meant fighting a battle. Ever since, cartoonists and audiences have associated donkeys with Democrats and elephants with Republicans.

POLITICAL PARTIES

Two political parties dominate US politics: the Democratic Party and the Republican Party. Both parties have changed significantly throughout US history. The modern Democratic Party is characterized by progressive policies. For example, Democrats want the government to protect individuals from being exploited by making and enforcing rules about how companies do business. They want the government to make businesses use environmentally safe processes to avoid damaging nature. Democrats argue for government programs that assist citizens struggling with issues such as poverty. Many Democrats support a move toward

Voting is one opportunity for eligible Americans to make their political opinions heard.

universal, or government-funded, health care. Democratic beliefs tend to appeal to voters who live in urban areas.

The Republican Party is characterized by more conservative policies. Republican values include limiting how much the government can intervene in the personal and professional business of Americans and prioritizing the government's role in fortifying a strong military defense. Republicans argue that health care is better managed by private businesses than by the government. Republicans believe that less of the government's tax revenue should be used for social services. Instead, they believe citizens should voluntarily donate to causes they support to help those in need. Republican beliefs tend to appeal to voters who live in rural areas.

All US citizens have their own mix of perspectives and beliefs. Many fall somewhere in between the Republican and Democrat platforms. US laws and governance represent both parties, and government leaders who disagree must meet to make compromises.

US SYMBOLISM

At the center of the United States' symbolism is the national flag. Many Americans place a lot of significance on their national flag. People may hang a US flag at the front of their homes, especially during national holidays such as Independence Day. A US flag always flies outside the White House in Washington, DC, where the president lives. In many public schools, children start their day by turning toward the flag and reciting the Pledge of Allegiance.

THE STARS AND STRIPES

The design of the US flag tells a story. The 13 equal horizontal stripes of red and white represent the 13 original colonies. The blue rectangle in the upper left corner contains 50 white stars to represent the 50 states. The flag has changed over time. The original flag, when there were only 13 states, showed 13 stars arranged in a circle to represent that all the states were equal. The color blue stands for loyalty, truth, justice, and friendship. Red symbolizes courage and zeal, while white represents purity and moral conduct.

The US national anthem, "The Star-Spangled Banner," is a tribute to the flag. Poet Francis Scott Key was inspired to write the lyrics when he witnessed the US flag still flying over Fort McHenry as the sun rose after a long night of brutal warfare in Baltimore, Maryland, during the War of 1812 (1812–1815). Today, almost every major sporting event begins with the playing of the national anthem, during which most people stand and face the flag with their hand over their heart.

A SYMBOL OF COURAGE AND STRENGTH

Eagles have long symbolized leadership and vision in folktales and legends. In 1782 the founding fathers designated the bald eagle as the national bird of the United States. In the country's coat of arms, an eagle holds an olive branch in one talon to signify peace and arrows in the other to signify military might. The bald eagle is so synonymous with the United States that it has its own day of celebration. Congress designated June 20 as American Eagle Day.

THE US MILITARY

Seven components make up the US military: the Army, Navy, Air Force, Marine Corps, Coast Guard, National Guard, and Space Force. Each has a specific job. Sometimes, the branches will work together in a joint operation.

In order to join the military, people must be US citizens or legal permanent residents, at least 17 years old, and able to speak, read, and write English fluently. A person must have earned a college degree to become a military officer. Some schools, such as the Citadel and West Point, focus specifically on training future military leaders. Most US universities offer Reserve Officers' Training Corps (ROTC) programs in which people can learn about and experience military life while pursuing a four-year degree of their choice. The program offers scholarship money in exchange for at least four years of military service upon graduation, depending on the branch of the military.

Historically not all troops have joined the military voluntarily. Conscription, also called the draft, has been used to summon men to war throughout US history. Conscription practices have changed over time, especially after the Vietnam War. Conscription ended in 1973, but all men aged 18 to 25 are still required to register with the Selective Service System for a potential future draft in a national emergency.

The military is organized in a hierarchical system that follows a strict chain of command. The president is at the top, serving as commander in chief. The US military has bases of operation in all 50 states as well as in dozens of other countries. The United States' two million military personnel and nearly 800,000 civilians make its military larger than the population of Chicago, the third-largest city in the United States.[3]

In 2023 the United States spent $916 billion on its military. The nation with the next-highest military budget, China, spent less than one-third that amount. US military spending that year was equal to 3.5 percent of the nation's gross domestic product (GDP), which is the value of goods and services created by a country in one year.[4] Several nations spent a higher percentage of their GDP on their militaries, including Saudi Arabia, Israel, and Russia. However, these nations' total military spending was still a small percentage of the US military budget. For example, Russia spent 5.9 percent of its GDP on its military in 2023.[5] That equaled approximately $109 billion.[6]

CHAPTER **SEVEN**

ECONOMICS

Although the US economy experienced some challenges due to the COVID-19 pandemic beginning in 2020, the state of the country's economy is strong and optimistic. The nation's GDP increased overall in the mid-2020s. This is a sign that the US economy is performing well. Businesses are earning money, so they hire more employees. Those employees earn more money, which they spend at other businesses. When unemployment is high and people have less money to spend, businesses don't earn as much and GDP decreases.

In 1791 the US government opened the First Bank of the United States. This organization printed money and served as the bank of the US government. However, many Americans disliked so much power being concentrated in one organization. They were

The New York Stock Exchange is a hub for economic activity around the world. Its platform allows people to buy and sell shares of companies, called stocks.

MINI **BIO**

ALEXANDER HAMILTON

Alexander Hamilton was a founding father and one of the figures who most influenced the early US economy. Hamilton attended school in the British North American colonies. He became involved with protests against British rule and served in the Continental Army during the American Revolution. He impressed his superiors so much that General George Washington invited him to be on his staff.

When George Washington was elected as the first US president, he tasked Hamilton with developing a financial plan for the country's new government. As the first secretary of the treasury, Hamilton wanted to help fund new industries in the United States by placing high taxes on goods from other countries. Influenced by the Bank of England, Hamilton argued for a central government bank.

With a national bank supporting it, the US government could establish a national currency and improve its global standing. Hamilton's plan became the First Bank of the United States. This bank collected taxes, stored government funds, and paid the government's bills. It paved the way for the Federal Reserve in place today.

Since 1929, Alexander Hamilton's portrait has been printed on the $10 bill.

concerned that the bankers who ran the First Bank would make policies that helped the elite and harmed farmers and other working-class people. Politicians debated for decades, testing different approaches, until they passed the Federal Reserve Act in 1913. The compromise led to the creation of 12 independently run regional reserve banks spread across the nation.[1] Together these form the Federal Reserve, the bank of the United States.

The Federal Reserve is a decentralized national bank, meaning that it is not one organization but many acting as one unit. Monetary decisions are made by a group of financial experts that represent businesses and citizens from every region of the United States. This structure helps distribute power and ensure that the bank's policies reflect the needs of people around the country.

The financial experts at the Federal Reserve are responsible for keeping the US economy strong and stable. They watch the markets and factors such as unemployment and GDP closely. When a sector of the economy is struggling, the Federal Reserve steps in to help guide the economy in the right direction. For example, the Federal Reserve may lower interest rates on loans, encouraging other banks to lower interest rates as well. This makes it less expensive for people and businesses to borrow money. This results in more spending and more hiring, which helps the economy.

The US dollar is the official currency of the United States. It is also the most commonly held reserve currency, meaning that it can be used for international trade. The US government prints its paper money in several denominations—$1, $2, $5, $10, $20, $50, and $100—and mints coins.

The median household income in the United States in 2023 was $80,610. That means half of Americans made more than this amount and half made less. The median income had increased 4 percent since the same study in 2022.[2] Across the states, incomes vary widely. In Washington, DC, the median household income was $108,210, while in Mississippi it was $54,203.[3]

Each year, the government estimates the income a family of four would need to live in the current economic climate. The amount varies by state and determines whether people can receive financial assistance from the government. In 2023 about 11 percent of people were living under the federal poverty threshold.[4]

The United States is a mixed economy, meaning that it mixes capitalist and socialist characteristics. Private ownership of businesses is allowed, and incomes vary widely. However, the government creates regulations to ensure fair treatment of employees and often enacts programs to help those with low income.

The government encourages and assists people opening their own businesses through the Small Business Administration. People with a business idea and a well-thought-out plan can receive advice and funding to get started. The US economy

THE AMERICAN DREAM

The American Dream is the idea that in the United States, every single person is entitled to the opportunity and freedom to pursue the life they choose. This principle stems from the first settlers who came to the land that would become the United States. They hoped to live free from the unfair systems that had held them back from practicing their chosen religions and improving their lives. The American Dream has come to represent the concept that anyone in the United States can achieve success if they set their mind on a goal and commit to consistent hard work.

relies on small businesses, since they make up more than 99 percent of all US businesses and are responsible for nearly 45 percent of the country's GDP.[5]

INDUSTRY AND RESOURCES

With abundant natural resources, the United States is home to many industries. The nation's fertile soil and various climates contribute to a vibrant agricultural industry. Fruits, vegetables, cotton, and tobacco are common exports.

Some areas of the United States are well-known for the agricultural products that are produced in them. The Dairy Belt, which stretches from New England to the Great Lakes region, is home to many farms raising cows, goats, and sheep. The conditions of the Great Plains are good for growing wheat, so it earned the name the Wheat Belt. The Corn Belt lies between the Ohio River and the lower Missouri River. Many farms there grow corn and soybeans. Several regions of the Southwest are home to cattle ranches. The tropical regions of the United States produce citrus fruits such as limes and oranges.

The United States contains 27 percent of the world's total coal reserves.[6]

Forestry—the management, cultivation, and harvest of trees and other plants—is a key industry in the dense forests of the Pacific Northwest. Many US resources are buried underground, and extracting them is another huge industry. Coal, iron, and nickel mined in the United States are exported around the world. Drilling for oil and natural gas is one of the biggest industries in the United States.

Some of the most popular job fields in the United States are in the sectors of technology, health care and pharmaceuticals, and logistics. The tech industry accounted for nearly 9 percent of the US GDP in 2023.[7] National health expenditures, or the amount of money spent on health-related activities and care, was 17.6 percent of the GDP in 2023.[8]

TRANSPORTATION AND INFRASTRUCTURE

Infrastructure, the systems and structures used for the functions of everyday life, is an important issue for many Americans. Roads, utility lines, water treatment plants, and schools need to be maintained, upgraded, and replaced in order for Americans to be successful and enjoy a high quality of life. A majority of Americans want more improvement to the nation's infrastructure. Roads and bridges need to be updated and widened for growing amounts of traffic. Fast, reliable internet needs to be

AMERICANS LOVE CARS

In the 1960s, comedian, actor, and talk show host Groucho Marx talked about "America's love affair of the automobile," an expression that has remained popular ever since.[9] While city planners argued for more walkable cities and mass transportation, car manufacturers and sellers publicized the image of the automobile as necessary to modern US life. With its vast roadways and many gas stations, the United States is built for large automobiles, which is why American-made vehicles are larger than those made in other countries. Today, US infrastructure makes it difficult for many Americans to get around without cars.

There are nearly two million farms in the United States.

available to the growing number of people using an ever-expanding array of devices. Outdated water lines and lead pipes need to be dug up and replaced. People and politicians are also pushing for the development of sustainable and energy-efficient infrastructure. It is important to keep the nation's systems and structures in good repair. Infrastructure projects also create jobs for those who complete the work.

The United States ranks thirteenth in the world in terms of quality of infrastructure.[10] Politicians tend to put off long-term infrastructure investments in favor of short-term spending priorities.

The Bipartisan Infrastructure Law has funded many infrastructure projects, including the construction of new bridges.

SUSTAINABILITY IS A GROWING TREND

With a growing interest in managing climate change, many people are arguing for greater advancements in sustainable infrastructure such as solar panels. Sustainable infrastructure incorporates more reliance on renewable resources. Young people especially argue for putting money into infrastructure that supports environmentally friendly travel options with less impact on natural spaces. Electric public transportation and solar-powered lights are two examples of sustainable infrastructure.

Many political leaders argue over how much money should be spent and how it should be spent, which slows down projects such as replacing lead water pipes, upgrading airports, and building more electric car charging stations. However, in 2021, Congress passed the Bipartisan Infrastructure Law, the largest federal investment in infrastructure in the nation's history, authorizing up to $108 billion for these projects.[11]

CHAPTER **EIGHT**

THE UNITED STATES TODAY

Diverse global heritages have come together in today's United States to create a unique multidimensional culture. Each region and state has its own story, cultures, and ways of life. Just as the United States shows its pride with Fourth of July fireworks, states, cities, and neighborhoods celebrate with block parties, carnivals, and gatherings. The State Fair of Texas is one example. As one of the largest state fairs in the United States, it "celebrates all things Texan" through Hispanic culture exhibits, Texas history presentations, and hands-on activities with livestock, among other offerings.[1]

Throughout the United States, life differs greatly for city dwellers and those who live in the countryside.

Celebrations in the US Southwest may include cultural performances such as ballet folklórico, a Mexican dance.

About 80 percent of Americans live in urban areas, with the country's most densely populated cities being New York City and Los Angeles, San Francisco, and San Jose in California.[2] Both rural and urban locations have stores, schools, and entertainment, but cities offer more options. People who live in large urban areas have more mass transportation options, more nonagricultural job opportunities, and access to more cultural events such as symphonies and museums. People in urban areas tend to fare better economically. Urban areas are also generally more diverse and more accepting of new cultures and beliefs.

Rural areas have their own benefits, such as less traffic congestion, crime, and pollution. Fewer people looking for homes results in a lower cost of living in rural areas, and houses and yards are larger. Many small-town residents report experiencing a strong sense of community as a result of knowing most of their neighbors.

Approximately two-thirds of households own their homes. The remaining one-third rent their homes.[3] Most Americans live in an immediate

HEALTH CARE

One industry that many Americans agree needs reform is health care. Americans pay high rates for health care compared with other countries. They also experience higher rates of disease and injury than people in other wealthy countries regardless of income level, race, or ethnicity. One reason for this statistic is that the complicated and expensive health-care system takes a toll on people's health. Patients delay or fail to schedule necessary treatments when they can't afford them. They suffer with pain while waiting for insurance companies to approve their treatments. Many political leaders are working on plans to improve the US health-care system, whether by making health care less expensive or by expanding options for government-funded health care.

family–based household, meaning that parents and children live in one household. It is common for extended family members, such as grandparents, aunts, or uncles, to live separately. Same-sex marriages have been legal across the United States since 2015 and made up about 1 percent of US married couples in 2021.[4]

About 20 percent of Americans have always lived in or near the community where they grew up.[7]

About 70 percent of Americans have full-time jobs, working at least 35 hours per week.[5] While more than 60 percent of workers must enter a physical workplace to complete a shift, about 14 percent work remotely. The rest have a hybrid schedule, meaning some days they work from home and some days they work at their physical workplace.[6] Many businesses in the United States are open from 9:00 a.m. to 5:00 p.m. Monday through Friday, and those are considered regular business hours. This provides many Americans with leisure time on weekends and weeknights to pursue their own interests. Some people spend time in nature camping, hiking, or fishing. Taking art and fitness classes, joining social groups based on shared interests such as book clubs, and playing on local sports teams are popular options for recreation.

EDUCATION

Local and state governments run a free public school system for grades one through 12, sometimes including kindergarten, with some funding provided by the national government. This is how the majority of American children are educated. Individuals can also send their children to private schools. These are privately funded educational centers that require tuition and are sometimes aligned with a specific religion. In 2021, 49.5 million students attended public schools, while 4.7 million attended private schools.[8] Parents can also choose to homeschool their children.

The United States requires that young people receive an education. States make more specific laws about the years of education a student receives. One area of concern is the disparity in the quality of education among people from different parts of the country. Some critics argue that children who live in more affluent neighborhoods receive better public education than those in poor districts. This problem arises because schools' funding is often determined by their local government's tax revenue, so the schools in the poorest regions receive less funding per student than schools in more affluent areas.

The United States places more focus than many countries on special education for students with disabilities. Students with disabilities may require additional support in school, and in recent years, public schools have done work to create inclusive classrooms that support all learners. This means that specialists will intervene and provide extra help for students who show signs they might be struggling with some aspect of learning, including social and emotional challenges.

After twelfth grade, students may continue on to higher education programs, known as post-secondary education. Home to some of the world's top universities and research institutions, the US higher education system includes more than 4,000 colleges, universities, and other institutions that allow students a wide variety of academic opportunities. About 62 percent of high school graduates pursue post-secondary education.[9]

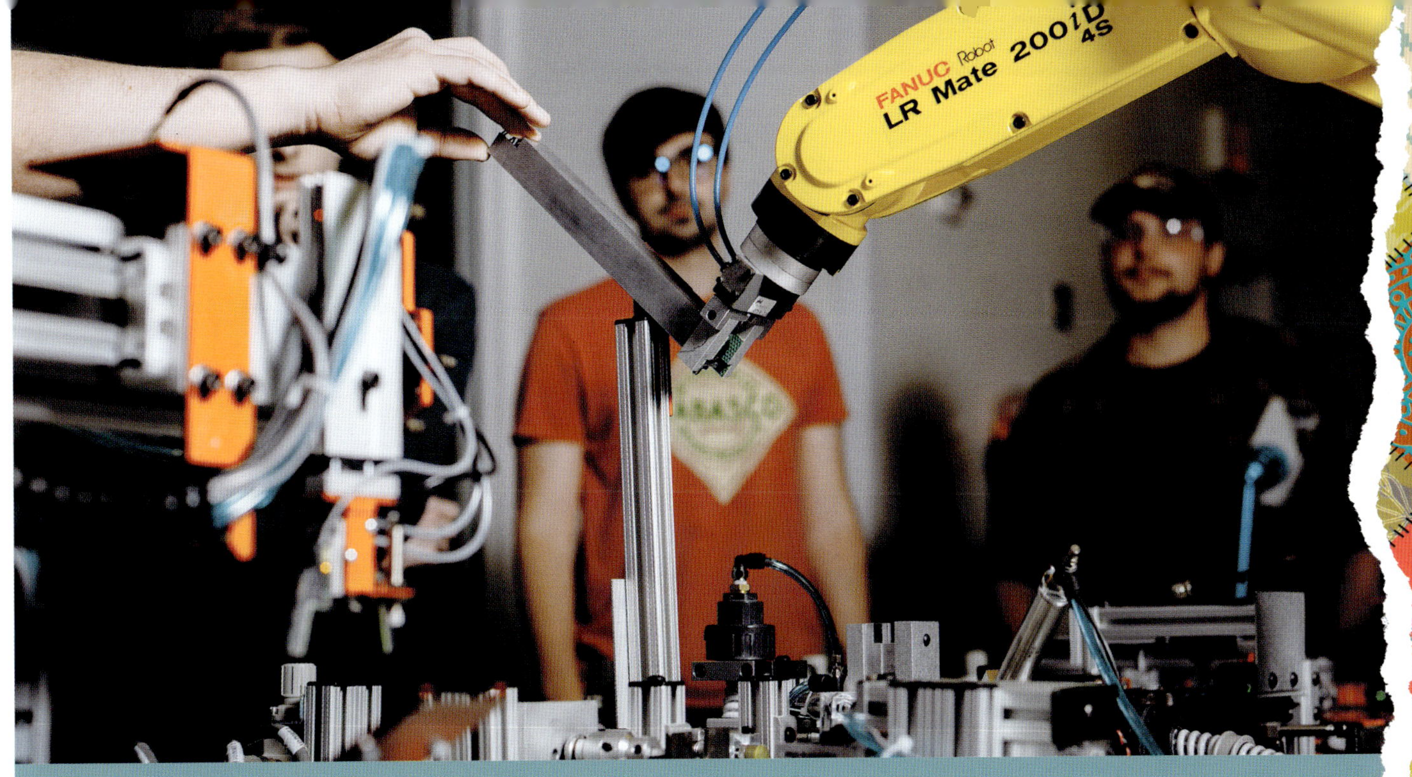

Many technical colleges teach courses in robotics. Students learn how to program, operate, and maintain robots.

Liberal arts schools specialize in arts, humanities, languages, and social and physical sciences. Institutes of technology offer state-of-the-art facilities for science, technology, engineering, and math (STEM) training. Trade schools offer students hands-on experience and licensure in careers such as automotive technology, carpentry, and cosmetology. Public institutions such as state universities and community colleges receive tax funding, although they still charge tuition. Private universities are funded only by tuition, donations, and endowments and may be more expensive than state schools.

Homelessness is a serious problem in the United States, and rates of homelessness are higher for people of color.

CHALLENGES TODAY AND IN THE FUTURE

Although many people view the United States as an example of hope and opportunity, the country also faces its share of challenges and tensions. One significant issue is racial inequality. Compared with white Americans, people of color have unequal access to housing, education, employment, and wealth. Many people argue that this is due in part to a history of racist policies and continuing discrimination in the United States. In 2023 white Americans were 30 percent more likely to own a home than Black Americans. Although national unemployment had improved since the COVID-19 pandemic sent it skyrocketing, 5.8 percent of Black Americans were unemployed compared with the national unemployment rate of 3.9 percent.[10]

High school completion rates for students of all races have risen in recent decades. However, the gap between these rates for white students and Hispanic students remains large, with less than 75 percent of Hispanic students completing high school compared with about 95 percent of white students.[11] Many lawmakers work toward racial equity by providing support systems for people of color and by introducing legislation that supports opportunities for all Americans.

Many political discussions are filled with competing, contradictory perspectives. Debates allow for voters to learn about and understand candidates' views. Discussions between individuals are also important opportunities to understand different perspectives. However, during the last 30 years, Americans have become more politically polarized, meaning their beliefs have moved away from the center toward the extremes. In addition, affective polarization, or the tendency to strongly dislike people with opposing views, has risen over the past decade, making election seasons more tense.

Political polarization makes it more difficult for people from different parties to discuss issues and reach a compromise. However, despite the appearance of rising political tensions, research shows that most Americans' views are more closely aligned than they believe. For example,

85 percent of Americans agree that the government should require background checks on people who buy guns through private sales.[12] Americans from both major parties want government entities to focus on reducing national debt. While the United States has always carried debt, the balance remained steady until it began rising dramatically in the 1980s.

LAND OF THE FREE, HOME OF THE BRAVE

Since its inception, the United States has fought and protected itself from interests that seek to harm it. In the modern day, technology provides additional avenues for extremist groups to seek influence in the United States. Some groups knowingly spread false information or conspiracy theories online, known as disinformation. Disinformation may be intended to deceive others, discredit politicians, or advance extremist agendas. It can confuse people about what sources they can believe. Experts study the patterns of sharing disinformation in an effort to curb the practice that is blurring the lines between facts and conspiracy.

THE RIGHT TO PROTEST

Throughout US history, public protests have been an important part of political activism and change. The First Amendment states that "Congress shall make no law . . . abridging the freedom of speech, or of the press; or the right of the people peaceably to assemble, and to petition the Government for a redress of grievances."[13] However, this amendment does not protect all forms of protest. Protesters may be arrested for actions such as gathering on private property without permission, threatening public safety, or blocking traffic. It is not a violation of the First Amendment if police use force when responding to such actions. If a protester believes a person or group infringed upon their rights, the protester can challenge the person or group through a lawsuit.

On January 6, 2021, political tensions reached an extreme when a mob stormed the US Capitol building to interrupt a congressional session certifying the results of the 2020 presidential election.

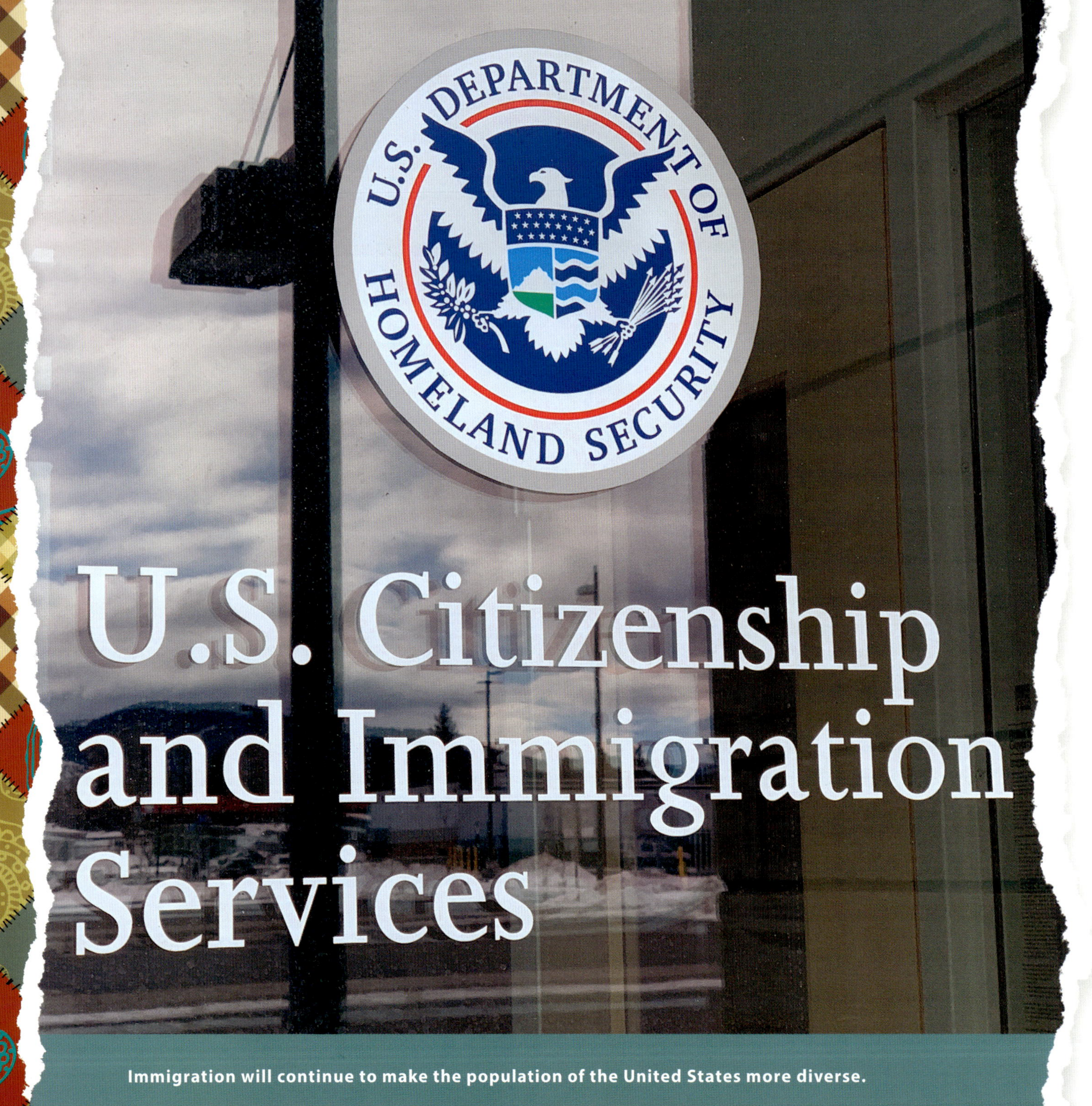

Immigration will continue to make the population of the United States more diverse.

THE GREAT AMERICAN NOVEL

In 1868 a writer named John William DeForest challenged Americans still grappling with national identity questions after the Civil War to write a book that encapsulated "the American soul."[14] He called the aspirational literary work the Great American Novel. However, no one author could ever explore the entire diverse American experience through a single Great American Novel. Hundreds of renowned literary titles capture elements of life in the United States, and new authors continue to explore US culture through both traditional and experimental books.

Still, the United States has endured a revolution, a civil war, two world wars, and several other serious conflicts and attacks. It is a nation of problem-solvers who look out for one another. Politicians and activists work to advance and expand the opportunities that make the United States a symbol of hope and prosperity.

Demographics in the country will continue to change over time. The US population is projected to skew older and more diverse than it is now. Urbanized areas will continue to adapt to the shifting needs of Americans. Technology will change how people live, work, and communicate. For more than 240 years, the United States has remained resilient. Americans can continue to stand as a shining example of what can be done when people work together as the world changes.

ESSENTIAL **FACTS**

OFFICIAL NAME: UNITED STATES OF AMERICA

GEOGRAPHY

Area: 3,796,742 square miles (9,833,517 sq km)

Highest Elevation: Denali at 20,308 feet (6,190 m)

Lowest Elevation: Death Valley at –282 feet (–86 m)

PEOPLE

Population: 342 million (2024 est.)

Most Populous City: New York (8.8 million)

Ethnic Groups: White, Hispanic, Black, Asian, Indigenous and Alaska Native, Native Hawaiian and other Pacific Islander, multiracial, other

Religions: Protestantism, Roman Catholicism, Judaism, Church of Jesus Christ of Latter-Day Saints, other Christianity, Islam, Jehovah's Witnesses, Buddhism, Hinduism, other, none

GOVERNMENT

Type of Government: Constitutional federal republic

Capital: Washington, DC

Head of State and Government: President

Legislature: Bicameral with a Senate and House of Representatives

ECONOMY

Currency: US dollar

Major Industries: Petroleum, steel, motor vehicles, aerospace, telecommunications, chemicals, electronics, food processing, consumer goods, lumber, mining

Natural Resources: Coal, copper, lead, uranium, gold, iron, mercury, nickel, silver, zinc, petroleum, natural gas, timber

NATIONAL SYMBOLS

National Anthem: "The Star-Spangled Banner"

National Bird: Bald eagle

National Flower: Rose

GLOSSARY

activism
Using vigorous campaigning to bring about political or social change through policy or action.

capitalist
Having to do with an economic system where businesses are privately owned and operated in order to make a profit.

colonize
To send a group of settlers to an area and assume political control of the area.

confederacy
A group of people, states, or other entities joined for a common purpose.

conscription
Mandatory enrollment in the military.

cultivate
To prepare and use land to grow crops.

development
Modification for human use, such as by building structures.

endowment
A large amount of money that has been given to an individual or an institution, such as a school or hospital, and is used to pay for its creation and continued support.

federal
Relating to a central government that holds limited power over a union of other governments.

interest rate
The amount of interest due per period on a loan, as a percentage of the amount borrowed.

loan
Money lent to an individual or company with interest.

plateau
An area of level ground that is higher than the surrounding area.

sovereign
Possessing the power to govern itself, as of a state or group.

stock market
A marketplace where people can invest in businesses by purchasing a small bit of ownership in a company, called a share.

ADDITIONAL **RESOURCES**

SELECTED BIBLIOGRAPHY

Murtoff, Jennifer. "American Dream." *Britannica*, 3 Sept. 2024, britannica.com. Accessed 20 Sept. 2024.

"Racial Economic Inequality." *Institute for Policy Studies*, n.d., inequality.org. Accessed 29 Oct. 2024.

"Slavery in America: The Montgomery Slave Trade." *Equal Justice Initiative*, n.d., eji.org. Accessed 26 Nov. 2024.

FURTHER READINGS

Mooney, Carla. *The Government Encyclopedia*. Abdo, 2023.

Rockler, Naomi. *American Democracy in Crisis*. ReferencePoint Press, 2024.

USA National Parks: Lands of Wonder. DK, 2024.

ONLINE RESOURCES

To learn more about the United States, please visit **abdobooklinks.com** or scan this QR code. These links are routinely monitored and updated to provide the most current information available.

MORE INFORMATION

For more information on this subject, contact or visit the following organizations:

iCivics
1035 Cambridge St., Ste. 1
Cambridge, MA 02141
vision.icivics.org
iCivics is an organization dedicated to teaching civic learning so that young Americans can improve their country for the future.

National Museum of American History
1300 Constitution Ave.
Washington, DC 20560
americanhistory.si.edu
The National Museum of American History in Washington, DC, hosts exhibits that explore the past and present of the United States. People can learn from the museum's collections in person or online.

National Park Service
1849 C St. NW
Washington, DC 20240
nps.gov
The National Park Service protects and maintains US national parks. It creates educational and recreational programs to encourage people to enjoy natural spaces.

SOURCE **NOTES**

CHAPTER 1. A TOUR OF THE UNITED STATES

1. "Nation's Capital Surges Past Pre-Pandemic Levels." *Washington, DC*, 29 May 2024, washington.org. Accessed 25 Nov. 2024.
2. "North Rim." *National Park Service*, 1 Nov. 2024, nps.gov. Accessed 25 Nov. 2024.
3. "Facts and Figures about the Bridge." *Golden Gate Bridge Highway and Transportation District*, n.d., goldengate.org. Accessed 25 Nov. 2024.

CHAPTER 2. GEOGRAPHY

1. Jesslyn Shields. "What Are the 7 Largest Countries in the World by Area?" *How Stuff Works*, n.d., science.howstuffworks.com. Accessed 25 Nov. 2024.
2. Caitlin Dempsey. "Alaska's Coastline Is Longer Than All the Other 49 States Combined." *Geography Realm*, 21 June 2021, geographyrealm.com. Accessed 25 Nov. 2024.
3. "Niagara Falls." *New York State Museum*, n.d., nysm.nysed.gov. Accessed 25 Nov. 2024.
4. "Chesapeake Bay." *National Wildlife Federation*, n.d., nwf.org. Accessed 25 Nov. 2024.
5. "North East Climate." *Climate Data*, n.d., en.climate-data.org. Accessed 25 Nov. 2024.
6. "America the Beautiful." *American Literature*, n.d., americanliterature.com. Accessed 25 Nov. 2024.
7. Elwyn B. Robinson and John L. Dietz. "Great Plains." *Britannica*, 17 Oct. 2023, britannica.com. Accessed 25 Nov. 2024.
8. "Great Lakes Ecoregion." *National Oceanic and Atmospheric Administration*, 1 Feb. 2019, noaa.gov. Accessed 25 Nov. 2024.
9. "Present Climate of the Midwest." *Teacher-Friendly Guides*, n.d., geology.teacherfriendlyguide.org. Accessed 25 Nov. 2024.
10. "Geologic Formations: How Badlands Buttes Came to Be." *National Park Service*, n.d., nps.gov. Accessed 25 Nov. 2024.
11. "The South." *Britannica*, 18 Nov. 2024, britannica.com. Accessed 25 Nov. 2024.
12. "Weather." *National Park Service*, n.d., nps.gov. Accessed 25 Nov. 2024.
13. John W. James and Armand J. Eardley. "Sierra Nevada." *Britannica*, 25 Nov. 2024, britannica.com. Accessed 25 Nov. 2024.
14. Armand J. Eardley and Richard A. Marston. "Rocky Mountains." *Britannica*, 17 Nov. 2024, britannica.com. Accessed 25 Nov. 2024.
15. "Climate and Weather on the PNT." *Pacific Northwest Trail Association*, n.d., pnt.org. Accessed 25 Nov. 2024.
16. "Alaska Weather and Climate." *Alaska.org*, n.d., alaska.org. Accessed 25 Nov. 2024.
17. "Climate of Hawaii." *Western Regional Climate Center*, n.d., wrcc.dri.edu. Accessed 25 Nov. 2024.

CHAPTER 3. PLANTS AND ANIMALS

1. "Biodiversity in Focus: United States Edition." *NatureServe*, 2023, natureserve.org. Accessed 26 Nov. 2024.
2. "Largest US Cities by Population 2024." *World Population Review*, n.d., worldpopulationreview.com. Accessed 26 Nov. 2024.
3. "Eastern Deciduous Forest." *National Park Service*, 23 Sept. 2024, nps.gov. Accessed 26 Nov. 2024.
4. "Denali." *National Geographic*, 19 Oct. 2023, education.nationalgeographic.org. Accessed 26 Nov. 2024.
5. "Size of the Redwoods." *National Park Service*, n.d., nps.gov. Accessed 26 Nov. 2024.
6. "The Rainforest." *Hawaii Tropical Botanical Garden*, n.d., htbg.com. Accessed 26 Nov. 2024.
7. "Largest Bird's Nest." *Guinness World Records*, n.d., guinnessworldrecords.com. Accessed 26 Nov. 2024.
8. "American Bison." *National Wildlife Federation*. n.d., nwf.org. Accessed 26 Nov. 2024.
9. "State Animal: California Grizzly Bear." *State of California Capitol Museum*, n.d., capitolmuseum.ca.gov. Accessed 26 Nov. 2024.
10. "National Park System." *National Park Service*, 16 Dec. 2024, nps.gov. Accessed 23 Dec. 2024.
11. "These Are the 10 Most Popular National Parks." *National Geographic*, 14 Nov. 2024, nationalgeographic.com. Accessed 26 Nov. 2024.

CHAPTER 4. HISTORY

1. Becky Raines. "New Data Suggests a Timeline for Arrival of the First Americans." *Oregon News*, 24 Feb. 2023, news.uoregon.edu. Accessed 26 Nov. 2024.

2. Elizabeth Prine Pauls. "Native American History." *Britannica*, 15 Nov. 2024, britannica.com. Accessed 26 Nov. 2024.

3. "Slavery in America: The Montgomery Slave Trade." *Equal Justice Initiative*, n.d., eji.org. Accessed 26 Nov. 2024.

4. "Louisiana Purchase." *Britannica*, 22 Oct. 2024, britannica.com. Accessed 26 Nov. 2024.

5. Elizabeth Prine Pauls. "Trail of Tears." *Britannica*, 10 Sept. 2024, britannica.com. Accessed 26 Nov. 2024.

6. "Mexican-American War." *Britannica*, 24 Oct. 2024, britannica.com. Accessed 26 Nov. 2024.

7. Rachel Nuwer. "Women Fought in the Civil War Disguised as Men." *Smithsonian Magazine*, 29 Apr. 2014, smithsonianmag.com. Accessed 26 Nov. 2024.

8. "US Participation in the Great War (World War I)." *Library of Congress*, n.d., loc.gov. Accessed 26 Nov. 2024.

9. "Great Depression Facts." *Franklin D. Roosevelt Presidential Library and Museum*, n.d., fdrlibrary.org. Accessed 26 Nov. 2024.

10. Ronald H. Spector. "Vietnam War." *Britannica*, 22 Jan. 2025, britannica.com. Accessed 27 Jan. 2025.

11. "Events of the Day." *9/11 Memorial and Museum*, n.d., 911memorial.org. Accessed 26 Nov. 2024.

12. "WHO COVID-19 Dashboard." *World Health Organization Data*, n.d., data.who.int. Accessed 26 Nov. 2024.

CHAPTER 5. PEOPLE AND CULTURE

1. "How Many People Are Coming to the US and Where Are They Coming From?" *USA Facts*, n.d., usafacts.org. Accessed 26 Nov. 2024.

2. "United States." *CIA World Factbook*, 19 Nov. 2024, cia.gov. Accessed 26 Nov. 2024.

3. "New Report on the Nation's Foreign-Born Population." *United States Census Bureau*, 9 Apr. 2024, census.gov. Accessed 26 Nov. 2024.

4. "United States."

5. "United States."

6. Tom Hale. "Why English Is Not the Official Language of the US." *IFL Science*, 22 Jan. 2024, iflscience.com. Accessed 26 Nov. 2024.

7. Matthew Smith. "20 Alaska Native Languages Now Official State Languages." *Alaska Public Media*, 23 Oct. 2014, alaskapublic.org. Accessed 26 Nov. 2024.

8. Sandy Dietrich and Erik Hernandez. "What Languages Do We Speak in the United States?" *United States Census Bureau*, 6 Dec. 2022, census.gov. Accessed 26 Nov. 2024.

9. "United States."

10. William O. Bright and Lyle Campbell. "Indigenous North American Languages." *Britannica*, 27 Oct. 2024, britannica.com. Accessed 26 Nov. 2024.

11. Lillian Sparks. "Preserving Native Languages: No Time to Waste." *US Department of Health and Human Services*, 15 Aug. 2015, acf.hhs.gov. Accessed 26 Nov. 2024.

12. "Statistics—Broadway in NYC." *Broadway League*, n.d., broadwayleague.com. Accessed 26 Nov. 2024.

13. "North American Sport Franchises." *Stadium Maps*, 17 Nov. 2024, stadium-maps.com. Accessed 26 Nov. 2024.

14. "Are Fewer Kids Playing Sports?" *USA Facts*, 21 Mar. 2024, usafacts.org. Accessed 26 Nov. 2024.

15. "How Much Sugar Is Too Much?" *American Heart Association*, 23 Sept. 2024, heart.org. Accessed 26 Nov. 2024.

SOURCE **NOTES** CONTINUED

CHAPTER 6. POLITICS

1. Jeanne Mason Fogle. "Washington, DC." *Britannica*, 25 Nov. 2024, britannica.com. Accessed 26 Nov. 2024.
2. "2024 General Election Turnout." *Election Lab*, 10 Dec. 2024, election.lab.ufl.edu. Accessed 27 Jan. 2025.
3. "How Many People Are in the US Military?" *USA Facts*, 21 Feb. 2024, usafacts.org. Accessed 26 Nov. 2024.
4. Einar H. Dyvik. "Countries with the Highest Military Spending Worldwide in 2023." *Statista*, 4 July 2024, statista.com. Accessed 23 Dec. 2024.
5. Aaron O'Neill. "Ratio of Military Expenditure to Gross Domestic Product (GDP) in Russia 2000–2023." *Statista*, 2 Aug. 2024, statista.com. Accessed 28 Jan. 2025.
6. "Military Spending in Eurasia 2021–2023, by Country." *Statista*, 25 Oct. 2024, statista.com. Accessed 28 Jan. 2025.

CHAPTER 7. ECONOMICS

1. "The Decentralized Structure of the Federal Reserve System." *US Government Accountability Office*, 17 Sept. 2019, gao.gov. Accessed 26 Nov. 2024.
2. Gloria Guzman and Melissa Kollar. "Income in the United States: 2023." *United States Census Bureau*, 10 Sept. 2024, census.gov. Accessed 26 Nov. 2024.
3. Katherine Engel and Kirby G. Posey. "Household Income in States and Metropolitan Areas: 2023." *United States Census Bureau*, Sept. 2024, www2.census.gov. Accessed 26 Sept. 2024.
4. Emily A. Shrider. "Poverty in the United States: 2023." *United States Census Bureau*, 10 Sept. 2024, census.gov. Accessed 26 Nov. 2024.
5. "The State of Small Business Now." *US Chamber of Commerce*, 10 Apr. 2023, uschamber.com. Accessed 26 Nov. 2024.
6. "United States." *CIA World Factbook*, 19 Nov. 2024, cia.gov. Accessed 26 Nov. 2024.
7. Ahmed Sherif. "Tech Sector as a Percentage of Total Gross Domestic Product (GDP) in the United States from 2017 to 2023." *Statista*, 11 Dec. 2024, statista.com. Accessed 23 Dec. 2024.
8. "NHE Fact Sheet." *Centers for Medicare and Medicaid Services*, 18 Sept. 2024, cms.gov. Accessed 28 Jan. 2025.
9. Eric Jaffe. "The Invention of America's 'Love Affair' with the Automobile." *Bloomberg*, 29 Jan. 2015, bloomberg.com. Accessed 26 Nov. 2024.
10. Patrick J. Kiger. "How Bad Is America's Infrastructure, Really?" *How Stuff Works*, n.d., science.howstuffworks.com. Accessed 26 Nov. 2024.
11. "Bipartisan Infrastructure Law." *Federal Transit Administration*, 16 Nov. 2023, transit.dot.gov. Accessed 26 Nov. 2024.

CHAPTER 8. THE UNITED STATES TODAY

1. "About Us." *State Fair of Texas*, n.d., bigtex.com. Accessed 26 Nov. 2024.

2. "Nation's Urban and Rural Populations Shift Following 2020 Census." *United States Census Bureau*, 29 Dec. 2022, census.gov. Accessed 26 Nov. 2024.

3. Tony Mariotti. "Homeownership Statistics." *Ruby Home*, 23 Aug. 2023, rubyhome.com. Accessed 28 Jan. 2025.

4. Carolina Aragão et al. "The Modern American Family." *Pew Research Center*, 14 Sept. 2023, pewresearch.org. Accessed 26 Nov. 2024.

5. "The Economics Daily." *US Bureau of Labor Statistics*, 5 Feb. 2024, bls.gov. Accessed 26 Nov. 2024.

6. Kim Parker. "About a Third of US Workers Who Can Work from Home Now Do So All the Time." *Pew Research Center*, 30 Mar. 2023, pewresearch.org. Accessed 26 Nov. 2024.

7. Kim Parker et al. "What Unites and Divides Urban, Suburban, and Rural Communities." *Pew Research Center*, 22 May 2018, pewresearch.org. Accessed 26 Nov. 2024.

8. "Education: K–12." *Policy Circle*, n.d., thepolicycircle.org. Accessed 26 Nov. 2024.

9. Melanie Hanson. "College Enrollment and Student Demographic Statistics." *Education Data Initiative*, 31 Aug. 2024, educationdata.org. Accessed 26 Nov. 2024.

10. "Racial Economic Inequality." *Institute for Policy Studies*, n.d., inequality.org. Accessed 26 Nov. 2024.

11. "Racial Differences in Educational Experiences and Attainment." *US Department of the Treasury*, 9 June 2023, home.treasury.gov. Accessed 26 Nov. 2024.

12. "Political Polarization in the United States." *Facing History and Ourselves*, 26 Aug. 2024, facinghistory.org. Accessed 26 Nov. 2024.

13. "Constitution of the United States." *Constitution Annotated*, n.d., constitution.congress.gov. Accessed 26 Nov. 2024.

14. "The Great American Novels." *Atlantic*, 14 Mar. 2024, theatlantic.com. Accessed 26 Nov. 2024.

INDEX

ABOUT THE **AUTHOR**

MARIE JASKULKA

Marie Jaskulka writes fiction and nonfiction for teens. She minored in American Studies and is fascinated by US culture, history, cuisine, and road trips. She once drove cross-country from Alaska through the Pacific Northwest to Seattle and straight across the Midwest to the East Coast. It took two weeks.